KS4
Citizenship Studies
The Study Guide

This book takes you through everything you
need to know for KS4 Citizenship Studies.

It covers the National Programme of Study, and the
OCR, Edexcel and AQA GCSE Short Course Specifications.

And then, in the spirit of going the extra mile, we've put in
a smattering of not-so-serious bits to try and make the
whole experience at least partly entertaining for you.

We've done all we can — the rest is up to you.

What CGP is all about

Our sole aim here at CGP is to produce the highest quality
books — carefully written, immaculately presented and
dangerously close to being funny.

Then we work our socks off to get them out to you
— at the cheapest possible prices.

Contents

Contents

Published by CGP

Contributors:
Katie Braid, Ben Fletcher, Rosie Gillham, Sharon Keeley,
Elisabeth Page, Lynda Turner, Dennis Watts

With thanks to Glenn Rogers and Pete Townsend for the proofreading.
With thanks to Jan Greenway for the copyright research.

Acknowledgements:
Page 5:
Whites only sign, Barry Lewis/Alamy
Nelson Mandela quote from Rivonia Trial, 1964
Nelson Mandela as President of South Africa, Eye Ubiquitous/Alamy
Page 72:
Voting turnout data from British Election Study, National Centre for Social Research; University of Essex.
Office of National Statistics. Reproduced under the Terms of the Click-Use Licence

Every effort has been made to locate copyright holders. If any copyright holder would like us to make an amendment to the acknowledgements,
please notify us and we will gladly make amendments upon reprint.

ISBN: 978 1 84146 965 2

Clipart from Corel®
Printed by Elanders Ltd, Newcastle upon Tyne.

Based on the classic CGP style created by Richard Parsons.

Your Rights and Responsibilities

So here we go, off on the merry path of citizenship-ness. And it's straight into a really juicy topic — rights and responsibilities. Everyone should know their rights — after all, knowledge is power my friend...

Rights give you Freedom and Protection

1) Everyone has rights — things that you're entitled to, or are free to do.
2) Rights are important because they make sure people are treated fairly.
3) Legal rights are set down in the laws of countries, e.g. the right to vote, or to be refunded for faulty goods. If you don't get your rights you can take the issue to court.
4) Your legal rights change as you become older and more mature. For example in England and Wales:

> *There are lots of types of rights:*
> *human rights — page 3*
> *political and civil rights — page 7*
> *moral rights — page 8*
> *social rights — page 8*

- At 14 years — you can: work part-time (you might be able to do some types of job at 13, depending on local laws, e.g. a paper round); enter a bar to buy soft drinks (big wow).

  > *Minimum ages are set by law to protect you and the rest of society.*

- 16 years is a biggie — you can: buy lottery tickets; leave school (once you've done your GCSEs); have heterosexual or homosexual sex (but only with people who are also at least 16 years old and agree to have sex with you); get married with your parents' consent.
- At 17 years — you can drive a car.
- At 18 years — you can: buy cigarettes; buy alcohol and drink it in public bars; vote in elections; make a will; leave home without parental permission; get married without parental or court approval; rent or buy a house and get a mortgage; go into a casino; buy fireworks; stand for Parliament as an MP.
- At 21 years — you can adopt a child, or stand for the European Parliament as an MEP.

5) Legal rights can differ between countries, e.g. in England, mothers have the right to take up to 39 weeks paid maternity leave from work. But in Sweden, they have the right to take up to 16 months.

But Rights Can't Exist Without Responsibilities

1) Responsibilities as a citizen are all about respecting the rights of others and doing what is expected of you.
2) Rights need to be balanced by responsibilities. For example:

Your responsibility to go to lessons and behave yourself.

Headteacher's/Governors' responsibility to set school rules and deal with persistent troublemakers.

YOUR RIGHT TO EDUCATION

YOUR TEACHER'S RIGHT TO A SAFE PLACE TO WORK

Your teacher's responsibility to keep up to date with their subject and teach you well.

Parents' responsibility to teach their children how to behave.

The responsibility of each adult to take an interest in politics and vote.

THE RIGHT TO LIVE ACCORDING TO DEMOCRATIC VALUES

3) Your responsibilities change as you get older too, for example:

- At 10 years you're expected to know the difference between right and wrong and can be charged with criminal offences if you break the law. (It's 8 in Scotland, but they're planning to raise this to 12.)
- At 18 years you are responsible for supporting yourself. This usually involves getting a job so that you can afford to buy the things that you need.
- If you have children of your own you become responsible for bringing them up. This includes feeding, clothing and housing them up to the age of 18.

Emma wished her mum wasn't responsible for clothing her — she picked such dodgy hats.

You have the right to not learn this page...

...but it's the sort of information that'll be dead handy in life, if not for your Citizenship project or your exam. So it's probably a good idea to get your head down and make sure you really understand it.

More on Rights and Responsibilities

So basically, there are rights and responsibilities pretty much everywhere you look. See, here are some more.

The Government is Responsible for Children's Rights

The United Nations Convention on the Rights of the Child (UNCRC) sets out rights for all children under 18. They include:

- the right to life
- the right to a name and nationality
- the right to have their best interests considered in matters that affect them
- the right to live in a family environment and to have contact with both their parents
- the right to healthcare, education and social security
- the right to leisure, culture and the arts

Little Betty could have done without her right to culture and the arts.

The UK government accepted this Convention in 1991, meaning that they have the obligation (duty) to make sure that every child gets their rights.

The government took this further with the Children Act 2004. This was the legal bit of 'Every Child Matters' — a government plan for improving things for children in the UK. The aim is for every child to enjoy life and be able to achieve their full potential, as well as being kept healthy, safe and free from poverty.

Rights and Responsibilities can be Different for Each Parent

1) By law, a mother always gets parental responsibility for her child. The father gets this responsibility too, as long as he's married to the mother when the child's born. Parental responsibilities include things like protecting the child, disciplining them and providing them with a home.

2) But, whether they're married or not, both parents are responsible for supporting their child financially. In some cases, this means the father has to pay for their child as they grow up, even though they don't have the legal right to see their child.

'Fathers4Justice™' were a pressure group that performed dramatic stunts to try to get equal rights for fathers (the most famous was climbing on to Buckingham Palace dressed as Batman).

3) Grandparents don't have any legal responsibilities for their grandchildren, but it can be argued that they have moral responsibilities, e.g. to intervene if the child doesn't have a loving, safe environment.

We Have Rights and Responsibilities in Our Relationships

Couples can legally formalise their relationships through marriage (a contract between a man and a woman) or civil partnerships (between a same-sex couple). This gives them additional rights and responsibilities. E.g:

- If the couple have children both partners automatically have parental responsibility for them. If a couple aren't married then only the mother has this responsibility automatically (see above).
- If the couple divorce then one partner may have to pay maintenance to the other, e.g. if one partner gave up work to bring up children then they may be entitled to financial support from their ex.
- The couple are accepted as each other's next of kin and are responsible for making medical decisions for their partner if he or she is unable to do so themselves, e.g. because they're in a coma.
- There are also some pension benefits for married couples.
- If one partner dies the other will inherit a large proportion of their money and possessions (they won't necessarily get everything unless a will has been made — some might go to children or other relatives).
- When one partner dies, the surviving partner won't have to pay inheritance tax on what they inherit.

Many people think that couples who live together have a 'common-law partnership', with the same rights as married couples and civil partners. This isn't the case — although they now have legal protection in several areas, they have far fewer rights than people who are married or who have a civil partnership.

You have a right to a name — but your parents are responsible for picking it...

My parents named me Sheep and I've never herd the end of it. Ewe'd think they'd broken some kind of rights law. Baaa with me, I've nearly got to the tip. Oh yes, here it is — learn this page. Useful, I know.

Human Rights

Human rights. Well, they're our _rights_ as _humans_, aren't they. Surely there can't be any more to it than that...

The United Nations Defined Human Rights in 1948

1) Human rights are the moral, legal and political rights that ought to apply to every human being on Earth.
2) Human rights are basic freedoms, such as freedom from violence and discrimination, or entitlements, e.g. to education or a fair trial.
3) The United Nations (UN) defined human rights in the Universal Declaration of Human Rights (1948). The aim was to lay down minimum rights for every person, in every country in the world.

The Universal Declaration Lists Human Rights

The Universal Declaration of Human Rights contains 30 specific sections (called articles). They cover lots of different rights. Here are some examples:

My favourite article is Article 26

Article 1 — All human beings are born free and equal in dignity and rights.
Article 2 — Everyone is entitled to all the rights outlined.
Article 4 — Everyone has the right to freedom from slavery.
Article 9 — No one shall be arrested, detained or exiled without good reason.
Article 11 — Everyone is innocent until proven guilty.
Article 19 — Everyone has the right to freedom of opinion and expression.
Article 26 — Everyone has the right to a free education.

Jamie loved his right to freedom of expression. The neighbours weren't so keen.

Human Rights are Enforceable by European Law

1) The Universal Declaration of Human Rights is a statement of the way things ought to be, but it means nothing in a court of law.
2) Other sets of rules on human rights are enforceable by law though. For example, the European Convention on Human Rights, which was passed by the European Union (EU) in 1953.

A convention is an agreement between a number of countries to follow the same law.

3) The European Convention on Human Rights is based on the Universal Declaration of Human Rights. A lot of the articles are similar, e.g. there are articles on the right not to be enslaved, the right not to be tortured and the right to have freedom of speech.
4) The Convention must be followed in all European Union countries.

The European Court of Human Rights in Strasbourg. (I think.)

5) If someone believes that they aren't getting their rights, they can take their case to the European Court of Human Rights in Strasbourg, France. But they need to try to get the matter resolved in their own country first.
6) The court includes 47 judges, one for each member of the Council of Europe. The judges are elected every six years.

There's also the European Charter

Yep, just to add further confusion, there's also the European Charter of Fundamental Human Rights (2000). This is based on the European Convention on Human Rights. It lists all the rights (political, social, etc.) that European citizens are entitled to in one place. It's meant to make it easier for people to find out their rights.

Article 968 — the right to not study Citizenship...
No, sadly, that one isn't in any kind of declaration or convention, or any other long-worded legal thingumajig. Shame. Well, as you don't have a legal leg to stand on, I'd suggest that you get on and learn this page.

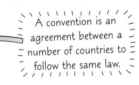

Protecting Human Rights

There's still a bit more on human rights you need to know I'm afraid, so settle yourself down and plough on...

British Law has the Human Rights Act 1998

1) Britain is a <u>member</u> of both the <u>UN</u> and the <u>EU</u>, so it's <u>signed</u> the Universal Declaration of Human Rights <u>and</u> the European Convention on Human Rights (see the previous page).

2) But these rights <u>weren't</u> part of the UK's domestic <u>law</u> — you had to go all the way to <u>Strasbourg</u> to claim your rights under the European Convention.

3) So in 1998, Parliament passed the <u>Human Rights Act</u>. It came into force in 2000, and <u>protects</u> the human rights of <u>British citizens</u> under <u>British law</u>. This makes it much easier (and cheaper) for British citizens to claim their rights.

The rights listed in the Act are pretty <u>similar</u> to those in the Convention.

> There are some grey areas though — for example, in 2004, an ex-prisoner (who'd been convicted of killing someone with an axe) challenged the British law that prevents prisoners from voting. He took the case to the <u>European Court of Human Rights</u>, which ruled that he was right — prisoners should <u>only</u> lose their right to liberty, and not any other rights. This put the British government under pressure to change the law.

4) The Human Rights Act has an effect at <u>all levels</u>, e.g. <u>local councils</u> and the <u>police</u> mustn't breach any laws set out in the Act, e.g. everyone must be presumed innocent until proved guilty.

5) Anyone who feels they're being denied their human rights can seek help and advice from the <u>Equality and Human Rights Commission</u> (EHRC). The EHRC is particularly interested in cases were there is an equality issue on grounds such as age, disability, race, religion or sexual orientation.

Frankenstein's new monster only had human rights.

International Humanitarian Law Protects Rights in Conflict

1) <u>International Humanitarian Law</u> applies to <u>armed conflict</u>. It's a set of international rules that regulate how wars are fought in order to <u>limit</u> the amount of <u>suffering</u> and <u>destruction</u> they cause.

2) The rules aim to <u>protect</u> the <u>human rights</u> of civilians, children and anyone not involved in conflict (like health workers or wounded soldiers). For example:

- weapons that create needless suffering (e.g. biological weapons) are not allowed
- attacks must be directed against the enemy forces and not towards civilians
- an enemy who surrenders must not be killed or injured
- anyone captured must not be tortured
- wounded soldiers must be cared for

> International humanitarian law is also known as the 'laws of war'.

3) The law is defined in the <u>Geneva Convention</u>, which has been signed by <u>194 countries</u>, including the <u>UK</u>. This means the UK's armed forces are responsible for following the rules and will be <u>punished</u> if they don't.

The International Criminal Court Tries War Criminals

1) In 1998 the <u>International Criminal Court</u> (ICC) was set up at <u>The Hague</u> in the Netherlands, to bring war criminals to justice.

2) War criminals are people who are responsible for their country or soldiers committing 'war crimes'. They're usually people in <u>power</u>, so they'd never be prosecuted in their own country.

> War crimes include <u>genocide</u> (killing a large number of a national or ethnic group, e.g. the Jews in World War II) and <u>crimes against humanity</u> (e.g. deliberately attacking or killing civilians).

So, all ISN'T fair in love and war then...

Ambulances or doctors showing a <u>red cross or red crescent</u> aren't allowed to be attacked. Nor is anyone waving a <u>white flag</u>. But you can't wear a red cross and wave a white flag, get close to the enemy, then attack them — this is against the laws of wars too. Wars are still very nasty though, even with these rules.

Campaigning for Rights

Common sense tells us that it's a good idea to know your rights. But sometimes people aren't given the rights that they should have. When this happens, some people may decide that they have to take action...

Sometimes People Have to Fight for Their Rights

People with very strong values or views often take action to win legal rights...

Example: Nelson Mandela

Nelson Mandela was a political activist in South Africa during apartheid.

Apartheid was a government regime of racial segregation.
Under apartheid, everyone was classified into racial groups, e.g. white, black, etc.
People who weren't white didn't have the same legal rights as those who were.

For example, non-whites weren't allowed to vote, they had to use separate schools and hospitals (that were usually lower quality), they couldn't travel freely through the country and they were often forced to move from their homes and away from their families.

Mandela felt very strongly that apartheid was wrong and he took action against the regime.
He joined an anti-apartheid group and organised demonstrations and campaigns to end apartheid.
He became a leader in the fight against apartheid and became well-known around the world.

Because of his actions he was arrested and put on trial for sabotage. At his trial he made a famous speech, outlining why he had taken the actions he had and showing how strongly he believed in the importance of equal rights for all South Africans, saying...

> During my lifetime I have dedicated myself to this struggle of the African people...
> ...I have cherished the ideal of a democratic and free society in which all persons live together in harmony and with equal opportunities. It is an ideal which I hope to live for and to achieve. But if needs be, it is an ideal for which I am prepared to die.
>
> Nelson Mandela, April 20th 1964, Pretoria, South Africa.

Mandela was convicted and spent 27 years in jail as a political prisoner. People all over the world campaigned for his release.

He was finally released in 1990, after intense pressure from within South Africa and abroad. Apartheid ended soon afterwards.

Nelson Mandela was elected President of South Africa in 1994, after the country's first multiracial elections. All South Africans now have equal legal rights, regardless of the colour of their skin.

Nelson Mandela isn't the only person who has taken action to win rights for people. For example:

- Emmeline Pankhurst campaigned for women's right to vote in the UK in the early 20th century — see page 7.
- Martin Luther King campaigned for equal rights for black people in the civil rights movement in the USA.
- Mahatma Gandhi, an Indian political leader, campaigned for India to be free from British rule.

Amnesty International Campaigns for People's Human Rights

1) Amnesty International UK is an organisation that runs campaigns to fight for people's human rights all over the world — especially prisoners of conscience (people put in prison just because of their race or beliefs).

2) It aims to educate the public and governments around the world about human rights and take action against specific cases of human rights abuses.

3) Anyone can join Amnesty International UK — members put pressure on governments by writing to them or publicly protesting. People can also help by donating money

(You gotta) Fight for Your Right (to Party)...

So spoke the ever-so-wise Beastie Boys. And many people would agree with them. Well, maybe not so much about the partying bit, but the general principle is right. If people throughout history hadn't fought for their rights then we'd live in a very different society. And it probably wouldn't be different in a good way...

Conflicts of Human Rights

So if we're all given our rights, everything will be peachy, yeah? Oh, if only it were that simple...

Not All Human Rights Have Equal Weight

The Human Rights Act separates human rights into three types:

1) ABSOLUTE RIGHTS — these are rights that you're always entitled to and that can't be withheld. For example, the right to life, the right to protection from torture.

2) LIMITED RIGHTS — rights that can be restricted under certain circumstances. For example, the right to liberty is restricted for people who've committed a crime and been put in prison.

3) QUALIFIED RIGHTS — these are rights that require a balance between individual rights and the rights of the community. For example, the right to respect for private and family life, and freedom of expression.

Everyone has the right to freedom of speech but it's an offence to stir up racial or religious hatred, as this infringes other people's rights to live free of abuse and fear.

This classification is useful when there is a conflict of human rights — when one person having their rights means that another person is denied theirs. In this situation rights have to be compromised. Absolute rights should never be compromised, but limited and qualified rights sometimes have to be.

There are Many Situations Where Human Rights Conflict

There are lots of situations that may lead to a conflict of human rights. For example:

DNA testing in crime reduction

- When someone is arrested a sample of their DNA may be taken. This sample may stay on police records even if charges against them are dropped or they are found not guilty of the crime.
- Some people think that under Article 8 of the Human Rights Act (the right to respect for private and family life) this shouldn't be allowed as it's an invasion of privacy of people who've done nothing wrong.
- However, some serious crimes, e.g. murders, have been solved by checking through records of DNA samples, so many people think that samples should not only be taken from suspects but that DNA testing should be compulsory for everyone. They argue that having DNA samples of everyone would help to protect people's lives (Article 2) and their possessions (Article 1 of Protocol 1).
- So in this situation the rights outlined in Article 8 of the Human Rights Act conflict with the rights outlined in Articles 1 and 2.

Publishing sensitive information

Paul didn't like to complain, but he wasn't convinced that his new identity as a 6-year-old Norwegian girl was the best.

- In 1993 two-year-old James Bulger was murdered by two ten-year-old boys — Jon Venables and Robert Thompson. Both boys were sentenced to jail and were released in 2001. To help them get on with their lives, they were given new identities.
- On their release some newspapers wanted to publish information on their new identities and location. They argued that they had the right to do this under Article 10 of the Human Rights Act (free expression).
- However, lawyers representing Venables and Thompson argued that publishing these details would put the boys at risk of harm or even death from members of the public, so going against Article 2 of the Act (the right to life).
- In this conflict of human rights a judge decided that the risk to the murderers' absolute right to life outweighed the newspapers' qualified right to freedom of expression, and banned the publication of details of the boys' new lives.

The right to education AND the right not to be tortured MUST conflict...

Human rights laws are there to protect our freedom but some people think they protect the wrong people, like criminals. When rights conflict, there has to be a compromise — so not everyone's going to be happy.

Political and Civil Rights

Political or civil rights prevent the government from having too much power over individuals.
They developed slowly to give us the democratic system that you'll soon come to know and love...

Democracy — Rule by the People

1) The UK is a representative democracy — the people elect representatives (Members of Parliament or MPs) to make the decisions that affect everyone. We vote to elect a national government every 5 years or so.

2) Since 1969, everyone over 18 has had the right to vote. (There are a few exceptions, e.g. many prisoners can't vote.) This is sometimes called universal suffrage.

> Universal — everyone's treated the same
> Suffrage — the right to vote

During the 19th and 20th centuries groups campaigned for this right.
Their protests eventually reformed the electoral system...

The democratic right to wave pom-poms. Don't underestimate it.

More and More People Gradually Got the Vote

Towards the end of the 17th century, parliament took control from the monarchy.
Before that, the UK was an absolute monarchy — the King or Queen had all the power.

In the 19th century, a series of REFORM ACTS led to all parts of the country being fairly represented in Parliament, and more and more men being allowed to vote.
(Only wealthy property owners could vote originally, and women definitely couldn't.)

The Representation of the People Act in 1918 meant all men over 21 and all women over 30 could vote.
The valuable contribution that women and men, rich and poor had made during World War I was recognised.

In 1928 the voting age for women was lowered to 21, bringing equality.

Here are some examples of groups that campaigned for these changes:

The Chartists were a working class movement that held strikes and demonstrations from 1838 to 1848. They wanted votes for all men over 21, secret ballots and annual elections. They fell out and gave up after they were unsuccessful.

The Reform League held demonstrations in 1866-1867. They were more successful than the Chartists.

Suffragists and suffragettes campaigned in the early 20th century for the right for women to vote.
They carried out direct action like chaining themselves to railings, and went on hunger strikes in prison.

Other Civil Rights Developed Too

Civil liberties came about as philosophers put forward their ideas, and laws were tested in court, e.g.

- In 1689 John Locke wrote that a government's power should not be unlimited, saying they should only have the power to protect people and their property. His arguments influenced the way many people thought.
- The Bill of Rights 1689 established political rights such as free and fair elections of MPs and freedom of speech within parliament.
- In 1882 the High Court upheld the rights of protesters to march — saying that the state didn't have the power to stop people doing anything not prohibited by laws. At the time, people were influenced by thinkers such as John Stuart Mill, who wrote in 1859 on the importance of freedom of speech, opinion and assembly.

There's more on these freedoms on the next page.

We all have the right to play in the sea — no, that's universal surferage...

Democracy is not just about allowing people to vote in elections. For a true democracy people must have:
freedom of speech, freedom of opinion and freedom of association. These are explained on the next page...

More Rights and Freedoms

We're so used to some things — such as being able to talk to whoever we like, and not having our mail opened and read — that we don't even think about them as <u>rights</u>. But they are...

We All Have <u>Rights to Freedom...</u>

Many rights involve <u>freedoms</u> — you need to know the importance of the two below.
They're both included in the <u>Universal Declaration of Human Rights</u> (see page 3) and are vital for <u>democracy</u>.

(1) Freedom of Speech and Opinion

1) This means you have the <u>right to think and speak your views and ideas openly</u>.
2) Without freedom of speech, we couldn't have <u>political debates</u> or a <u>democratic system of government</u>.

(2) Freedom of Association

1) This means you have the <u>right to get together</u> with <u>who you like</u>, to do what you want (unless it's illegal).
2) It has loads of applications — from allowing people to chat to who they like down the pub, to allowing them to hold <u>peaceful protests</u> and form <u>political parties</u> — which is vital in a <u>democracy</u>.
3) Being able to join a <u>trade union</u> is an important part of freedom of association. Trade unions try to improve the conditions of employment for their members — groups of people have a better chance of <u>bringing about change</u> than individuals.
   (This was particularly important before workers' rights were protected by laws.)
4) However the right to join trade unions is limited, e.g. <u>police forces</u> don't have the right to <u>strike</u> (for obvious reasons).

"It's OK, I'm on strike today..."

Privacy is a Right Too

1) You have a <u>right to a private life</u> (e.g. people can't enter your home without your permission or read your letters. No one can take pictures of you when you'd expect privacy either).

2) Your <u>personal information</u> is confidential too. The <u>Data Protection Act 1998</u> means companies can only use it for certain things — and they can't pass it on without your <u>permission</u> (usually by getting you to tick a tiny box).

<u>CCTV</u> is used a lot in the UK for <u>crime prevention</u> and <u>detection</u>. But some people think that having so many cameras about is an <u>invasion of their privacy</u>.

3) Your privacy is <u>allowed to be invaded</u> by government intelligence in the interests of <u>national security</u>, e.g. detecting terror threats by tapping your phone (although phone tap evidence <u>isn't allowed in court</u>).

4) If someone's right to privacy is <u>infringed</u> the matter can be taken to court. E.g. the model Naomi Campbell won a privacy case against the Mirror newspaper after they published photos of her allegedly leaving a drug addiction meeting. But it's a matter of debate whether celebrities have a <u>lesser right to privacy</u> than the rest of us.

There are also Moral and Social Rights

1) <u>Moral rights</u> are based on a sense of <u>right and wrong</u>, e.g. the right not to be tortured, or to not have your property taken away without good reason. They should be the same in all countries.

2) <u>Social rights</u> are things like the right to education, to work, and to housing, health care and food.

3) Some social rights are provided by the <u>state</u> to help everyone get the best out of life. The government has gradually given the public <u>more</u> social rights, e.g:
   - The <u>1870 Education Act</u> provided <u>education</u> for children aged 5-12, and if you were poor it was <u>free</u>.
   - In <u>1908</u> the government passed the <u>Old Age Pensions Act</u>, giving an income to people too old to work.

Freedom from exams — oh please, please, please...

Well no, frankly, that's just not possible 'cause then you wouldn't be having to read this lovely revision book. I've worked so hard on it, I don't want it to go to waste. So go on, please learn this page — just for me. Ta.

Consumer Rights

Consumer rights — you have the right to consume a chocolate biscuit with this page.

Consumers and Businesses both have Rights

The rights of consumers and businesses compete and conflict because they each want different things — consumers want to buy quality goods or services for the lowest possible price, whereas businesses want to produce quality goods or services as cheaply as possible and sell them at the highest price that people will pay, to make as much profit as they can. So legal rights are given to both parties to make things fairer.

A Contract of Sale is Made When You Buy Goods

When you buy goods or pay for a service, a contract of sale is made between the business and the consumer — even though you don't usually sign anything.

Ray's new hands-free umbrella did not match what he expected.

| The consumer pays or promises to pay money for the goods. |  | The business is responsible for providing goods to the standard the consumer expects. |

The Contract is Broken if the Goods Don't Match Reasonable Expectations

If either party fails to deliver on their side of the deal then the contract is broken:

- the business has the right to get their goods back if they're not paid for.
- the consumer has the right to get their money back if the goods don't meet standards (see below).

Consumer Rights Have Legal Protection

It's not fair if you get faulty, shoddy goods, so your rights are protected by law.

E.g. the Sale of Goods Act 1979 says that...

- Goods must be of a decent quality and not damaged or faulty.
- Goods must be fit for purpose and do what the manufacturer claims they will.
- Goods must match the description given on the packaging.

Other laws say that businesses must be honest about their goods (e.g. Trade Descriptions Act 1968) and that goods must comply with safety standards (Consumer Safety Act 1987).

It means that if you buy goods that aren't up to scratch, you have the right to return them within six months and get a refund, a replacement, or the goods repaired.

But if you take the goods back after six months, you might not get a refund unless you can prove that the goods were faulty when you bought them (and not just because you dropped them).

Various Organisations Can Help with Your Consumer Rights

We're all pretty good at grumbling about how the new whatsit 'doesn't do what the ad said it would', or how the thingumajig broke as soon as you looked at it... but actually knowing when you're entitled to your money back is a different matter. Luckily, there are some organisations out there that'll help you.

Statutory bodies are funded by the government, for example:

- Consumer Direct — a service that gives advice on consumer issues.
- Office of Fair Trading — a government department that'll take action if consumer laws are broken.

Non-statutory bodies are independent advice agencies, for example:

- Citizens' Advice Bureau (CAB) — a charity that provides free advice on consumer rights (and other stuff).
- 'What Consumer' — a website offering consumer advice and forums, owned by a private company.

I definitely ordered jokes — this must be a faulty page...

If the Emperor had realised today that his new clothes were, well, not there — he'd have the right to get his money back or receive some clothes that lived up to the contract. See, it's useful stuff. But it doesn't cover everything — if you just change your mind about your new waterproof towel, then it's tough luck.

Rights at Work

Unless you're posh and loaded you'll spend more than half of your life <u>at work</u> earning money to support yourself — so it's important to know your rights in the <u>workplace</u>.

So many jobs... I wish I was a...

You have Rights at Work...

When you get a job you generally sign a <u>contract</u>. This lists <u>your</u> responsibilities and the responsibilities of <u>your employer</u>. Having these all agreed in writing should help prevent you being treated unfairly.

But whatever your contract says, there are some <u>laws</u> that affect how you're treated.

MINIMUM RATES OF PAY Nearly all workers are entitled to be paid the <u>minimum wage</u> — this varies according to <u>age</u>. If you're paid over a certain amount, you'll usually have <u>tax</u> and <u>National Insurance</u> deducted from your wage by your employer.

<u>Minimum rates of pay from 2011:</u>
£3.68 per hour for 16-17 year olds,
£4.98 per hour for 18-20 year olds and
£6.08 per hour for anyone 21 or over.

DISCRIMINATION <u>Most discrimination</u> in the workplace is <u>illegal</u> — it's illegal to pay <u>men</u> more than <u>women</u> because of their gender or to employ a <u>white</u> person instead of a <u>black</u> person just because of their skin colour. It's also illegal to discriminate on grounds of <u>age</u>, <u>disability</u>, <u>religion</u> or <u>sexuality</u>.

...builder...

...grape picker...

BUT people of a certain race, age or gender can sometimes be specially recruited for a job. E.g.:
* a part in a film might need to be played by a <u>young</u>, <u>Asian woman</u> for the film to make sense.
* a job promoting the welfare of a particular ethnic community might be done best by someone from the <u>same ethnic background</u>.

...water-skiing flag deliverer...

SAFETY <u>The Health and Safety at Work Act (1974)</u> outlines some of the <u>duties</u> that employers have, to keep their employees <u>safe</u> at work — e.g. the duty to provide any information, training and supervision that employees need to do their job safely.

...but you also have Responsibilities to Your Employer

1) Employers have to treat you fairly or they can face legal action and a hefty fine. But this works both ways. You can't just sit about all day, doing your nails and making long-distance phone calls. <u>You</u> have a <u>responsibility</u> to your <u>employer</u> too.

2) If you don't do your job properly (as set out in your <u>contract</u> or <u>job description</u>), your pay could be cut or your boss can even decide to fire your sorry ass.

3) You've also got to behave yourself with your <u>fellow workers</u>. If you're found guilty of <u>discrimination</u>, <u>bullying</u> or <u>harassment</u> you can be taken to court.

4) Employer and employee rights can <u>conflict</u>. E.g. an employer may have the right to say what employees <u>wear</u>, but employees might have the right to follow their <u>religious beliefs</u> by wearing, e.g., a turban.

Ricky wanted more laws against age discrimination.

You Can Join a Trade Union — But You Don't Have To

1) Whatever your job, there'll be a <u>trade union</u> you can join. E.g. teachers can join the National Union of Teachers and firefighters can join the Fire Brigade Union.

2) Trade unions help workers negotiate <u>fair pay and conditions</u>. They also provide <u>legal support</u> for members who've been unfairly treated.

If a union can't resolve an issue by negotiation, they might call for <u>industrial action</u> (e.g. a strike or a 'go-slow').

3) In the UK, you have the <u>right</u> to join a trade union. But you <u>don't</u> have to — it's entirely up to you. Your employer <u>isn't</u> allowed to treat you unfairly because of your decision.

"My greatest ambition, since I was a child, is to retire..."

So said George Sanders — the Brad Pitt of the 1950s. Incidentally, he didn't enjoy retirement at all, and committed suicide in the 1970s on the grounds that he was bored. Sad but true.

Landlord and Tenant Rights

Oooh, a page on the rights of the former Time Lord, David Tennant. Oh, it doesn't look like it's him...

You have Rights as a Tenant — and as a Landlord Too

A tenancy agreement is a contract (either verbal or written) that sets out the rights and responsibilities of both the tenant and the landlord. Tenancy agreements can't be ridiculously unfair because certain rights are protected by law. Here are the sorts of things you might find on a tenancy agreement...

If you're a tenant moving into a property...

If you're a landlord renting out a property...

You must keep paying rent for the first six months, whether you stay for that long or not.

You must pay the agreed amount of rent on time each month.

Your deposit covers any damage to the property.

You mustn't break any rules stated in the contract.

You need permission to do anything like painting the walls.

You have the right to live somewhere safe and not dangerous to your health.

This tenancy agreement is made between the Landlord and the Tenant on 15 September 2010.
Property address: 123 Weeroff
                    Timbuktu
                    CU L8R
1)   The lease runs from 01 October 2010 until 01 April 2011, after which one month's notice is required to end the agreement.
2)   The Tenant agrees to pay rent of £500 per month, on the first of every month.
3)   The Tenant agrees to pay a deposit of £250, which will be returned at the end of the tenancy if no damage is found.
4)   The Tenant must not keep any pets or have paying guests in the property.
5)   The Landlord must approve any alterations made to the property.
6)   The Landlord must maintain the property to a reasonable living standard and pay for any structural repairs.

You must let the tenant stay for the agreed length of time, and give notice before chucking them out.

You can only increase the rent if you give the tenant notice.

You must return the full deposit — unless your property is damaged beyond wear and tear.

Your property must be safe to live in (e.g. no dodgy wiring) and not cause health problems (e.g. breathing problems due to dampness).

You must look after the structure of the property (e.g. repair a leaky roof, or unblock a gutter) and make sure the essential services are available (e.g. water, gas and electricity supplies).

You can get Information and Advice from Various Bodies

If things go wrong, there are organisations you can go to for help. If action needs to be taken (e.g. to evict an unlawful tenant) then it's a civil law matter (see p. 39) for the county courts.

Statutory bodies are set up by the government to give advice, for example:

1) Directgov — a government information website, full of advice and online services (www.direct.gov.uk).
2) Local councils — provide information and advice on private renting and council housing.

Non-statutory bodies are businesses or charities that provide advice, for example:

1) Citizens' Advice Bureau (CAB) — a charity service that provides free information and advice.
2) Solicitors — qualified people who will give you advice and help you go to court if necessary. There's a (usually pretty hefty) charge, but some legal help is free to people on a low income.
3) The Ombudsman Service — a free, fair and independent service that will investigate complaints.
4) Shelter — a charity that helps people affected by a bad housing situation or homelessness.

I, the Tenant, hereby agree to host parties for everyone...

My advice: make sure you know what you're agreeing to. If anything looks dodgy, seek some better advice. Landlords and tenants both have rights to make it fair — so no one has to own or live in a ruined property.

Quick Test

This is really fundamental stuff, all about the way <u>all</u> human beings should expect to be treated — for no better reason than that they're human.

Deep.

But it's <u>also</u> about making sure you know all the 'Rights and Responsibilities' stuff you're expected to know for Citizenship. And that's where this page of questions will come in very handy indeed. Treat it as a <u>mini quiz</u> and see how much you know. The questions are in the order of the section to help you <u>check</u> your answers and <u>reread</u> any bits that didn't quite soak in properly the first time.

Away you go...

1) Give one right and one responsibility that a 14-year-old has.

2) Give one right and one responsibility that a teacher has.

3) How old do you have to be to be able to vote in an election?

4) How old do you have to be to be able to stand for Parliament as an MP?

5) At what age do you take criminal responsibility if you break the law?

6) Name two documents that set out children's rights.

7) If a couple aren't married, who automatically gets parental responsibility?

8) What is meant by the term 'human rights'?

9) What is the main difference between the Universal Declaration of Human rights and the European Convention on Human Rights?

10) Name the British equivalent of the European Convention on Human Rights.

11) What does International Humanitarian Law protect?

12) Why is an international court necessary to deal with war criminals?

13) How did people's rights differ during apartheid in South Africa?

14) Give an example of how Nelson Mandela fought against apartheid.

15) Name two other well-known people who have fought for people's rights and state what they fought for.

16) What type of right is the right to life? a) absolute, b) limited, c) qualified

17) Give an example of a qualified right.

18) Which type of right should never be compromised?

19) Why do some people think that it is an abuse of human rights for police to keep samples of DNA?

20) Briefly outline how the right to vote developed.

21) Name two freedoms that are essential for democracy.

22) What is a 'contract of sale'?

23) What does the Sale of Goods Act 1979 say?

24) Where could you go to get advice on consumer rights?

25) How old do you have to be to be paid a minimum wage?

26) Give an example of illegal discrimination in the workplace.

27) What kind of things does the Health and Safety at Work Act 1974 cover?

28) Name one responsibility that an employee has to their employer.

29) What sort of stuff could a trade union do to help you?

30) Do you have to join a trade union?

31) What is a tenancy agreement?

32) Where could you go to get advice on landlord and tenant rights?

Action in the School Community

A wise man once said, "with great power comes great responsibility". Well, you probably don't have great power, but you do have responsibilities, and, as the saying doesn't go, responsibility starts at school.

The School Community Includes Many Different People

1) The school community is made up of everyone who is involved with school life.

2) Some members of the school community may be involved with the school on a daily basis, e.g. pupils, teachers, teaching assistants, administrative staff, caretakers, technicians, cleaners and catering staff.

3) Others may be involved less directly or less frequently, e.g. parents, governors and local authority officers.

4) How well a school community functions depends on how much time and effort is put into improving it.

Pupils Can Help to Develop the School Community

Pupils are often the most influential group when it comes to determining the character of the school community. So it's really important that individual pupils get involved in improving school life. There's a wide range of actions that they can take. For example:

JOINING A SCHOOL COUNCIL

Your peers are other students.

A school council (sometimes called a student council) is a group of students who are elected by their peers to discuss issues affecting the life of the school and its pupils and to try to find solutions to any problems. There are many benefits to having an active school council, for example:

- It opens channels of communication between pupils and staff and allows pupils' voices to be heard.
- It can act as a springboard for new ideas and initiatives that will benefit the whole school community, e.g. peer mentoring schemes.
- Pupils can gain practical experience of democracy by running for school council. This could involve making speeches, campaigning and forming policies.
- School council members can develop their decision-making and team-working skills.
- Being on a school council gives students useful experience to put on job or college application forms.

HOLDING A POSITION OF RESPONSIBILITY

Many schools have opportunities for pupils to take on extra responsibilities and represent, guide or lead other pupils, e.g. as head boys/girls, prefects, monitors, house captains or captains of sports teams. Some schools may also encourage pupils to help out with younger children in the school, e.g. by running clubs or acting as mentors.

TAKING PART IN SCHOOL ACTIVITIES

Pupils can help to improve their school communities by getting involved in school groups and activities, e.g. school concerts, choirs, sports teams, extracurricular activities, etc.

SUPPORTING OTHER PUPILS

All pupils can get involved in school life by supporting their peers, e.g. by going to watch school concerts and plays or supporting sports teams.

A popular after-school activity: coloured ball lifting.

Spend more time at school to enjoy it more — errr... hello?!

You spend the best part of 12 years at school — and that's just if you don't go to sixth form. Even if you don't feel particularly community-spirited, it's worth getting involved with things just to break up the tedium.

Community Involvement

Wherever you live, getting <u>involved</u> with your <u>community</u> will help to make it a <u>better place</u>. Awww...

The <u>Local Community</u> *Includes All the* <u>People</u> *in your* <u>Area</u>

1) A <u>community</u> is a group of people who all have <u>something in common</u> —
    e.g. people who belong to a sports club, or who follow a particular religion.

2) Your <u>local community</u> is made up of everyone who <u>lives</u> or <u>works</u> in your <u>local area</u>.

3) So it includes <u>you</u>, your <u>family</u>, nearby <u>friends</u> and <u>relatives</u>, <u>shop workers</u>, <u>GPs</u>, <u>police</u> — loads of people.

4) How <u>pleasant</u> your local community is depends on how much <u>time</u> and <u>effort</u> is put into improving it.

<u>Improve</u> *your Community by Getting* <u>Involved</u>

There are <u>loads</u> of things you can do to make your community a <u>happier</u> and <u>healthier</u> place to live.
Like... you could do some <u>voluntary work</u>, get involved in a <u>community project</u> or do something for <u>charity</u>.

Voluntary work

1) Doing <u>voluntary</u> work means giving up your <u>time</u> and <u>skills</u> for free.

2) This could be helping to pick up <u>litter</u>, clean out a <u>pond</u>, run <u>children's activities</u>, <u>shop</u> for an elderly neighbour... it all helps to <u>improve community spirit</u> and make your area a <u>nicer</u>, <u>cleaner</u> place to live.

3) You get a lot out of being a volunteer too, like <u>meeting new people</u> and <u>learning new skills</u>.
    It's also great for getting <u>experience</u> to put on college application forms and gives you a chance to see what type of work you'd enjoy as a <u>career</u>.

Community projects

1) Community projects benefit from getting as <u>many</u> people <u>involved</u> as possible.

2) <u>Fund-raising events</u> are a good way of getting people to <u>join in</u>, like raising money to start a <u>project</u> or buy special <u>equipment</u>. E.g. the local community centre might be looking a bit <u>tatty</u> so everyone in the community decides to take part in a <u>sponsored donkey ride</u> to raise some cash to spruce it up a bit.

3) Many local councils run <u>action projects</u>, like <u>tree-planting</u>, to help encourage <u>wildlife</u> and make the area look <u>pretty</u>, for the benefit of everyone.

4) Some areas have schemes where you can visit <u>children in hospital</u> or <u>elderly people</u>, helping to make them feel <u>part</u> of the community.

5) <u>Youth clubs</u> run many <u>activities</u> and get young people <u>involved</u> in their communities.

The fashion-conscious volunteer would only plant flowers that didn't clash with her dress.

Charities

1) Lots of things that affect the local community are problems for the wider community too, e.g. <u>pollution</u>, <u>poverty</u> and <u>homelessness</u> are major issues on a national and global scale.

2) By getting involved with charities, like <u>Children in Need</u>, <u>Comic Relief</u>, <u>Oxfam</u> or <u>Friends of the Earth</u>, local communities can help to <u>raise awareness</u> and <u>raise money</u> to deal with issues that affect everybody.

3) <u>Community Service Volunteers</u> (CSV) are a UK volunteering charity. They organise national <u>Make a Difference Day</u> — the UK's largest single day of volunteering, where people across the country volunteer to <u>make a difference in their communities</u>.

There's more on helping communities around the world through charities on page 29.

Cheddar Alert — this is pure cheese...

No one's expecting you to build a school in Africa — not while you've got your GCSEs to study for anyway.
But get <u>involved</u> in your community and you can help to make a <u>difference</u>... it may be cheesy but it's true.

Pressure Groups

However much community work you do, say planting trees, you might find that the situation isn't improving much, e.g. because loads of other trees are still being chopped down. So you might fancy joining a pressure group and campaigning on the issue...

Pressure Groups Try to Influence Decisions

1) A pressure group is a group of people who are concerned about a particular subject or issue.
2) They campaign to get things changed — there's lots about the methods they use on the next page.
3) Pressure groups may be:

- Environmental groups such as Greenpeace, an international organisation that has campaigned against things like nuclear power, and tried to stop whale hunting by blocking whaling ships.
- Welfare groups, e.g. the RSPCA, which campaigns against animal cruelty in the UK, and Amnesty International, which campaigns to protect human rights all over the world.
- Groups that campaign about one particular event or issue. E.g. the Stop the War Coalition, which campaigns against the wars in Afghanistan and Iraq, or a local group campaigning to stop a particular hospital from closing.

The pressure group 'Get Dressed in the Dark' only had five members.

Interest Groups Represent Groups of People

Interest groups are pressure groups that promote the concerns of a section of society, e.g. farmers.

1) Trade unions like the NUT (National Union of Teachers) and professional organisations like the Law Society (which represents solicitors) represent the views of their members on issues like pay and working conditions, and campaign to change government policies that affect their members.
2) The government often consults with certain groups, called 'insider groups', to get their advice, e.g. the British Medical Association (which represents doctors) advises the government on its health care policies.
3) Consumer Organisations try to protect people from unfair prices and faulty goods — see page 9.

Campaigns can Succeed if Enough People Agree

Campaigners have to show governments that the decisions they want would be popular with voters.
For example:

1) In 2009, nearly all of the villagers living near the site of a proposed 'eco-town' in Leicestershire voted against it in a council poll.
2) The plan was for 15 000 'carbon-neutral' homes with power and heat from a waste wood power plant and wind farms.
3) Local people felt there would be too much traffic, not enough schools to go round, and that it would spoil the countryside.
4) A group called CASCET campaigned against the eco-town. They encouraged people to write to their MP, and got their points of view reported in the national news.
5) Later that year the housing minister decided not to approve the plan.

1) In 2005 celebrity chef Jamie Oliver delivered a petition to 10 Downing Street. It had been signed by 271 000 people who wanted school dinners to be improved.
2) The petition and the publicity surrounding it led to some processed foods being banned by councils.
3) The government also promised more money for school kitchens.

The designer of the new 50 kg burger was not popular with Jamie Oliver.

Queen are my favourite 'Under Pressure' group...

Pressure groups often try to show politicians that issues are important to lots of people. They don't always get the changes made though — there are two sides to stories, and only so much money to go round.

Pressure Groups — Tactics and Targets

Pressure groups try to get things <u>changed</u> — how they do this depends on what they're fighting for.

Pressure Groups want to Influence a Target Group

Pressure groups need to get the attention of the people with the power to <u>bring about change</u> — these people are their <u>target group</u>.

An early pressure group from Liverpool.

1) Pressure groups might target the <u>GOVERNMENT</u> for a change in <u>policy</u>, e.g. <u>Greenpeace</u> are campaigning for the government to stop developing <u>nuclear weapons</u>.

2) Pressure groups might target <u>BUSINESSES</u> for a change in <u>business practice</u>, e.g. <u>Nike</u> have been targeted with campaigns against using <u>sweatshop labour</u>.

3) Pressure groups target the <u>MEDIA</u> to <u>publicise</u> their campaign. This helps to <u>raise public awareness</u> of the issue and can mean <u>bad publicity</u> for the government or businesses (which neither want).

4) Pressure groups target the <u>PUBLIC</u> to make sure they <u>know</u> about the issue and will hopefully <u>support</u> the campaign. They might want the public to <u>donate</u> money to the cause, <u>vote</u> for a political party that'll tackle the issue, or <u>boycott</u> certain products (refuse to buy them).

E.g. many campaigns encourage people to boycott Nestlé products because of the way it markets milk formula in poor countries (it's thought to mislead mothers into believing formula is better for their babies than breast milk).

Different Tactics are Used for Different Campaigns

1) Pressure groups use a <u>range of approaches</u> to get their <u>messages</u> across.

2) Some methods involve <u>direct action</u> — doing something that people can't help but notice. E.g.:

Marching and Demonstrations
These involve people <u>coming together</u> in large numbers to <u>attract attention</u> to their issue, often by carrying banners. E.g. 225 000 people marched through Edinburgh in 2005 to draw attention to the Make Poverty History campaign.

BAN SMOKING

Publicity Stunts
These are often dramatic to capture the <u>media's</u> attention. E.g. <u>Fathers4Justice</u>™ were famous for their stunts — see page 2. <u>Greenpeace</u> built a big wooden ark on Mount Ararat to highlight the need to tackle climate change.

Strikes and Disruptive Demonstrations
These often prevent businesses from operating, so the demonstration can't be just ignored. E.g. people have <u>chained</u> themselves to <u>trees</u> that are going to be cut down, lorries have caused <u>traffic congestion</u> by driving slowly in protest at high fuel prices, <u>Royal Mail</u> workers have gone on <u>strike</u> to protest against changes to their working conditions.

3) Other methods are classed as <u>indirect action</u>. E.g.:

Lobbying Members of Parliament — <u>persuading</u> MPs to support your campaign. An MP can then raise the issue in <u>Parliament</u> on <u>your behalf</u>. E.g. you could lobby your local MP to protest against a hospital ward being closed down.

Petitioning — petitions let people in <u>power</u> know that a large number of the public share a view on an issue. E.g. Jamie Oliver petitioned for school dinners to be improved (see previous page).

Propaganda — using information <u>persuasively</u> and focusing on <u>certain facts</u>, say in material such as leaflets. Propaganda will almost certainly be biased — see page 58.

Letter-writing — <u>writing</u> to people in <u>power</u> to <u>raise the profile</u> of your campaign. E.g. many letters are written by members of <u>Amnesty International</u>, which helps to put officials under pressure to <u>stop human rights abuses</u> across the world.

Use of celebrities — when <u>celebrities</u> front campaigns, it increases <u>media publicity</u> and helps <u>influence</u> public opinion. E.g. <u>Women's Aid</u> uses celebrities like <u>Kate Thornton</u> and <u>Anna Friel</u> to raise awareness of <u>domestic violence</u>.

Propaganda — having a really good look at something...

The key to a successful campaign is to get people to <u>take notice</u>, <u>agree</u> with you and <u>bring about change</u>. But sometimes things get taken too far, destroying property and threatening lives, e.g. animal rights extremists have been known to plant bombs in labs that do animal testing. Again, everyone's rights have to be balanced.

Influencing Decision-Making

Some issues are <u>hot topics</u> — there are strong arguments on <u>both sides</u>, and all sorts of groups have an <u>interest</u>. <u>Public debate</u> on these issues is important to make sure that the <u>fairest</u> decisions are made.

Animal Experimentation *is Mainly Used in* Medical Research

1) <u>Millions</u> of animal experiments are carried out in the UK each year. Most are on <u>rats and mice</u>, but a few use <u>primates</u> (mostly monkeys for research on <u>brain</u> and <u>immune system diseases</u>).

2) <u>New drugs</u> and <u>medical treatments</u> are tested on animals to see if they work or have bad side effects <u>before</u> they're tested on <u>humans</u>. Animals are also used for research to better understand <u>biology</u>.

3) <u>New chemicals</u>, e.g. in foods or pesticides, are also tested on animals to see if they are <u>harmful</u>. But <u>cosmetics</u> can no longer be tested on animals in the UK, following <u>campaigns</u> by <u>animal rights groups</u>.

- <u>Opponents</u> such as <u>Animal Defenders International</u> say that <u>no animals</u> should be experimented on. They argue that it is <u>unethical</u> (morally wrong) and <u>unreliable</u> (because if a medicine works on an animal, it doesn't guarantee that it will work on a human). They want <u>alternative methods</u> to <u>replace</u> animal experiments.
- Groups such as <u>People for the Ethical Treatment of Animals</u> have filmed undercover and <u>exposed</u> laboratories that have <u>broken rules</u> on how animals should be treated. <u>Media coverage</u> of films like these has led to <u>prosecutions</u> and tighter restrictions.

- Groups such as the <u>Royal Society</u> (which represents scientists) campaign <u>for</u> animal research, arguing that almost every <u>medical advancement</u> in the 20th century relied on the <u>use of animals</u> in some way.
- <u>Religions</u> including Christianity and Islam permit animals to be used for <u>human benefit</u>, as long as <u>unnecessary suffering</u> is <u>avoided</u>.

Early hair transplant tests using schoolchildren were unsuccessful.

4) The <u>government</u> position is that medical advancement that might <u>save human lives</u> is <u>more important</u> than the <u>suffering of animals</u> used for research. <u>Plans</u> for experiments involving animals must show that <u>alternative methods</u> (e.g. using computer simulations or cells) would <u>not work</u>, and <u>suffering</u> is <u>minimised</u>.

Suspected Terrorists *can be* Detained Without Charging **Them**

1) Someone who's <u>arrested</u> must be <u>charged</u> with an offence (see page 42) or <u>released</u> after <u>24 hours</u>. This can be extended to up to <u>96 hours</u> by a magistrates' court, if the police can show it's necessary.

2) Following incidents like the <u>bombings</u> in New York on September 11, 2001 and London on July 7, 2005, the time that people <u>suspected of terrorism</u> can be <u>held without charge</u> has been extended to <u>28 days</u>.

3) Some people are strongly against this, while others feel it's necessary:

FOR:

The <u>Metropolitan Police</u> argue that they need <u>more time</u> to hold terrorist suspects because:
- evidence on terrorism plots takes a <u>long time to gather</u>.
- they sometimes have to arrest people to <u>prevent</u> a terrorist attack, before they've managed to gather <u>evidence</u>.

AGAINST:

- <u>Human rights</u> charity <u>Liberty</u> opposes this change. They argue that it's <u>inhumane</u> and infringes <u>human rights</u>.
- Some MPs opposed the change too — they said that the job of <u>Parliament</u> was to <u>protect rights</u>, not take them away.

4) The government has tried several times since to <u>extend detention time</u> further (to 90 days, and then to 42 days), saying that it's necessary to keep the UK <u>safe</u> from <u>terrorist attack</u>. But MPs from <u>all</u> political parties voted against it, so the Bill didn't get very far.

90 days' detention — that homework must have been seriously late...

Make up your own mind on these issues — there are no right answers. The government has to balance public opinion (which varies enormously) with the advice they get from scientific groups and the police.

Presenting Arguments

There are campaigns nearer to home (or rather, school) that you can get involved in...

Everyone is Entitled to Their Own Viewpoints

1) Everyone has their <u>own values</u>, <u>viewpoints</u> and <u>opinions</u>, which will be different to everyone else's.

2) Whatever you think, you need to be able to <u>express</u> your viewpoint clearly and <u>explain your reasons</u>.

3) You need to know the <u>different sides</u> of an argument so that you can <u>critically evaluate</u> your viewpoint
   — weigh up the evidence and explain why you still think that your viewpoint is right.

4) You might need to put yourself in someone else's shoes and argue for a viewpoint you <u>don't agree with</u>.

Debates are Used to Evaluate Viewpoints

A debate is a <u>serious discussion</u> about a particular issue. It allows people to put across their <u>opinions</u> to an audience and try to <u>win their support</u>. Debates give people the chance to <u>make up their own mind</u> and <u>vote</u>.

> Debates involve:
> * An impartial <u>chairperson</u> who keeps order and helps the debate to flow smoothly.
> * <u>Speakers</u> (or teams of speakers) who put across their viewpoints.
> * An <u>audience</u> who listen to the debate, ask questions and sometimes take a vote at the end.

1) The chairperson starts the debate by reading out the <u>motion</u> (the issue to be debated).

2) The speaker who <u>supports the motion</u> has a <u>limited</u> amount of time (e.g. three minutes) to argue <u>for</u> the motion.

3) Then the <u>opposition</u> speaker has the same amount of time to argue <u>against</u> the motion.

4) E.g. "*Should there be a further increase in university tuition fees?*"

Arguments FOR	Arguments AGAINST
• University education is a privilege, not a right. Graduates tend to earn more money so they'll be able to pay back any loans borrowed to pay the fees. • The costs of running universities are rising as more people want to get a degree. This uses public money that could be spent on things like hospitals and schools. • Even if tuition fees rose, getting a degree here would still be cheaper than in many other countries.	• Article 26 of the Universal Declaration of Human Rights says that everyone has the right to a free education. This should apply to university education too. • Students from well-off backgrounds can afford to go to university, but high fees discriminate against those from poorer backgrounds. • Most university graduates will contribute towards society, e.g. as doctors, teachers, engineers. This will balance out the money that was spent educating them at university.

5) Sometimes speakers <u>answer any questions</u> before each summing up their argument in a <u>closing statement</u>.

6) The chairperson may call for a <u>vote</u> from the audience — this could be a show of hands or a secret ballot. The <u>votes are counted</u> by the chairperson and the motion is announced as <u>carried</u> (won) or <u>failed</u> (lost).

Prepare Properly for Taking Part in a Debate

1) **Research the topic** — you need to get your <u>facts right</u> if you want to convince people with your argument. Use a <u>variety of reliable resources</u> to do your research, not just one biased or out-of-date website.

2) **Plan and practise your argument** — it'll give you more <u>confidence</u> when speaking. Make sure you present your argument in a <u>logical order</u> and practise it so that you're less likely to forget the <u>key points</u>.

3) **Know the other side of the argument** — someone will argue <u>against</u> your point of view so if you know what they're going to say, you can be ahead of the game and <u>prepare your response</u> to their argument.

> ### I don't mind public speaking — it's the public listening I struggle with...
> If you hate the thought of speaking your opinions in front of everyone then <u>don't worry</u> — you're not alone. Spend time <u>practising</u> your speech <u>out loud</u>. Yes you'll feel stupid, but it'll get you ready for the <u>real thing</u>.

Quick Test

You might be feeling a bit green around the gills after all the caring and sharing in this section, but don't write it off as touchy-feely schmaltz. Being a good citizen isn't hard and, shock horror, might even be a laugh at times. That doesn't mean you have to go out and get involved in every community scheme going — but putting something back into society makes things better for you and everyone else — which has got to make you feel good. And if you have to do some kind of campaigning for your project, then the pressure group stuff might come in handy too (though if you get told off for building another big wooden ark on Mount Ararat next to Greenpeace's, don't say I told you to).

Anyhow, have a go at the questions below, and reread any topics you're a bit shaky on.
Then go out and help grannies across the road and stuff.

1)   What is meant by the term 'school community'?

2)   Who are your peers?

3)   What is a school council?

4)   What is: a) a community?
                      b) your local community?

5)   Give three ways you can help your local community.

6)   How can you help other communities across the world?

7)   What is a pressure group? Give an example and say what they do.

8)   What is a trade union? What about a professional organisation?
       Give an example of each, and say what they do.

9)   Briefly describe two pressure group campaigns that were successful.

10)   Name four groups that pressure groups might target their campaigns towards.
       Explain why they might choose each group.

11)   What is the difference between direct and indirect action?

12)   Briefly describe a couple of methods of direct action, with an example of each.

13)   What is: a) propaganda?
                      b) lobbying?
                      c) boycotting?
                      d) petitioning?
                      e) really annoying?

14)   Give an example of a protest that affected government policy.

15)   Give an argument for and an argument against the use of animals in medical research.

16)   Give an argument for and an argument against extending the amount of time that
       suspected terrorists can be imprisoned without being charged.

17)   What's the point of knowing the reasoning behind a viewpoint you disagree with?

18)   What is a debate?

19)   What is the role of the chairperson in a debate?

20)   What is a motion in a debate?

21)   Name three things you should do to properly prepare for speaking in a debate.

The Economy

The economy is basically all about money and goods circulating through businesses and consumers...

The Economy — it's all about Buying and Selling

The economy is made up of people and organisations trading goods and services for money.

1) To make the economy work, people need to have something that other people want, like you want a nice pie, the baker wants your money — easy. Sometimes people barter — exchange goods for goods, or services for services, but we normally hand over money for what we want.

2) The economy is split into the public and private sectors:

THE PUBLIC SECTOR

- The public sector includes things like the army, the police force, and most schools and hospitals.
- Public means that they are owned by the government, and paid for out of taxes, for the benefit of everyone.

THE PRIVATE SECTOR

- The private sector contains all the businesses owned by private individuals.
- Private means that these businesses are funded privately, and are run for the benefit of the people who own them, as well as their customers and employees.

Private Businesses Drive the Economy

Private businesses are good for the economy both locally and nationally:

1) Private businesses boost local economies by providing jobs. People with a steady income have more money to spend. This encourages more service industries in an area, which in turn creates more jobs.

2) All businesses pay corporation tax on their profits. Corporation tax makes up about 10% of the government's revenue every year and helps pay for public sector services. So private businesses essentially pay for the public sector.

The Government Tries to Help the Economy do Well

1) The government is the country's main decision-making organisation for the economy. It uses different policies to try and make the economy grow.

2) The economy grows when the country produces lots of goods and services. So the government can help by, e.g:
   - investing in businesses and training people.
   - lowering tax rates, so people and businesses have more money to spend.

   > E.g. VAT was temporarily reduced from 17.5% to 15% in 2009 to try and boost spending.

3) But factors like the world economy, government policy or wars can lead to economic uncertainty.
   - This can reduce demand for goods and services, so there's less money for businesses to earn. Businesses that don't make enough money to pay their labour costs have to make people unemployed.
   - With people and businesses spending less, the economy can shrink and slump into a recession.

Having a Job is Good for You and for the Community

1) Earning money means you have some to spend — this gives you more freedom and control over your life.

2) When you spend money, the people and businesses that receive it can use it to pay wages to others.

3) You'll also be able to pay taxes, which helps the government to help everyone — see the next page.

4) When you save money, banks can lend it to people and to businesses.

5) Having a job is good for your self-esteem — which means you feel good about yourself:

   > When strangers meet, one of the first questions they usually ask each other is, "What do you do for a living?" Being able to give an answer like mechanic, hairdresser or doctor makes you feel you have a clear purpose in life.

An economy drive — travelling in a Reliant Robin...

It's easy to think of the economy as a big complicated mess that only people in suits should know about. But it's actually not that bad — it's mainly just buying and selling patterns, and the stuff that affects them.

Taxes

Nobody likes having their hard-earned cash taken away from them as tax. But in theory, you should see tax money again because it's supposed to be spent on public services, like schools — great.

The Government Raises Money Through Taxes

The government needs to raise money to pay for public services — and most of this comes from taxes.

Direct tax is charged directly out of your income, e.g:

1) Income tax and National Insurance are deducted from your salary and interest on savings. The more you earn, the more you pay.
2) Inheritance tax is collected from part of the amount of money left to someone in a will.
3) Capital gains tax is collected from your profit when you sell stuff like buildings, land or company shares.
4) Corporation tax (see previous page) is collected from the profits of businesses.

Indirect tax is charged on things that you buy, e.g:

1) VAT (Value Added Tax) is added to the price of many goods and services.
2) Excise duty is an extra tax on the price of alcohol, tobacco, petrol and diesel (to try to discourage people from buying them).
3) Road tax is an excise duty for using public roads — people driving low CO_2 emission cars aren't charged, but those driving gas guzzlers pay a hefty price.

No one wants to give away their cash — but these are meant to be fair ways of collecting taxes from people who can afford to pay them.

Taxes are Used to Pay for Public Services

The government spends taxes on providing important services so that they're available to everyone. Some big examples are:

- The National Health Service (NHS) — free healthcare for everyone.
- Social security and welfare — pensions and benefits for the unemployed and people unable to work.
- Education — free education up to the age of 18.
- Defence — like the army, navy and air force.

Local governments (town and county councils) collect council tax — the more your home is worth, the more tax you pay.
Council tax is spent on your local services, for example:

Local governments also get money from central government, business rates, and through parking charges.

- local schools
- the police service
- regular rubbish collections
- maintaining roads and footpaths
- leisure facilities

Deciding How to Spend Taxes is Really Difficult

1) The government tries to make taxation and spending as fair as possible for everyone. But it's a tricky task... there's only so much money to go round and you can't please everyone.

> E.g. some people think that we should spend more money on better equipment for the army, to save soldiers' lives. But other people think that this money should be spent on healthcare, instead of fighting wars in other parts of the world.

2) You need a balance between taxing people and businesses a fair amount that they can afford, and providing high quality public services.

3) The government selects a Chancellor of the Exchequer to make the difficult decisions about tax rates and spending plans. The Chancellor decides how the money from taxes will be divided up between things like health, education, defence and welfare.

4) If the government wants to increase spending in one area, say education, then more money needs to be raised — either by raising taxes or by cutting public spending in another area, such as health. Or, money could be borrowed, although interest has to be paid on this, which usually leads to increasing taxes in the future.

If you think algebra and quadratic equations are hard...

... then try juggling the demands of the country — no thanks, Mr Exchequer, it's all yours. It's a tough job — especially when a new government comes into power to find the previous guys left them with big debts to pay off, services to sort out, businesses to help, banks to bail out... Nope, I'll stick to my day job I think.

HARROW COLLEGE

The Global Economy

Each country's economy is linked into the global economy through trade. About 80% of the world's wealth is controlled by the richest 20% of its population. Hang on a sec, that doesn't sound very fair to me...

There are Global Inequalities of Wealth... for many reasons

1) Countries can be broadly classified according to how economically developed they are — richer countries are called More Economically Developed Countries (MEDCs) and poorer countries are called Less Economically Developed Countries (LEDCs).

2) Most MEDCs tend to be found in the north of the world, e.g. the USA and European countries. Most LEDCs are found in the south, e.g. countries in South America and Africa.

3) There are loads of factors that might make one country poorer than another, for example:

Geographical differences — every country has a different climate and different natural resources. This makes it really hard for some countries to develop, e.g. some African countries suffer from severe drought, which makes farming very difficult.

Political instability — some countries have suffered years of unstable or corrupt governments, even civil war. This often means they haven't invested money in the right things, such as education, so economic development is very difficult.

LEDCs Trade with MEDCs... but they're in a Cycle of Debt

1) During colonial times, most of today's LEDCs were ruled by MEDCs — the LEDCs tended to produce and supply raw materials, whilst the MEDCs developed new industries and markets.

2) Even when LEDCs gained independence, most of the trade links continued in this way.

3) Many LEDCs have tried to break away from being dependent on MEDCs by borrowing money (from banks in MEDCs or the World Bank — see the next page) to pay for their own country's development.

Although this money was often used for other things — such as supporting the luxurious lives of dictators.

4) When interest rates rose in the 1980s, most LEDCs couldn't afford to pay the interest on the loans. Their debts rose and they had no money to invest in agriculture, industry, healthcare or education, leading them into a 'cycle of debt'.

5) In the late 1990s, many lenders started cancelling debt on humanitarian grounds, to give LEDCs a chance to develop.

6) But some people think it's unfair for one country to borrow a lot of money from another and never have to pay it back.

Interest on the debt cannot be paid

Further loans required

Cycle of Debt

The debt grows as interest increases

The borrowing country becomes poorer

Some Countries Have Broken this Dependency Cycle

Some LEDCs have developed and benefited in the global economy.

For example, some LEDCs in South-East Asia, like South Korea, used to provide a cheap labour force for American and Japanese companies.

But they managed to break the dependency cycle by investing in infrastructure and specialising in high-tech products, and they've seen dramatic levels of industrialisation in the last few decades. Countries like this are now NICs — Newly Industrialised Countries.

That's SO unfair — what about MY debt...

Hmmm, you see there are always two sides to an argument. You might think rich countries should just be nice and help out their poor neighbours. But then, maybe it's unfair for one country to borrow lots of money and not have to pay it back. As usual, it's up to you to decide what you think about the whole big mess.

Globalisation

Globalisation — the process of making the world into one big happy family... awww...

Globalisation is when Economies become More Integrated

1) Globalisation is the process of all the world's economies becoming integrated to form a single community.

2) It happens as countries trade with each other more and more, so rely on each other's resources or services.

3) Multinational companies usually base their factories in poorer countries, where labour is much cheaper. Head offices tend to be in richer countries, where people have business skills and a better education.

4) Globalisation has increased as transport links and ICT have improved, making international trade easier.

Good points...	Bad points...
• Globalisation creates jobs in loads of countries, including poorer ones. • Money is spent in poorer countries, e.g. improving transport networks. • Countries do what they're best at, e.g. supplying cheap labour.	• But globalisation causes job losses in countries like the UK, as more and more things are being made elsewhere. • Employees in poorer countries are still paid low wages, even though companies make huge profits. • Globalisation leads to increased pollution as goods and resources are transported overseas.

Some International Organisations Promote Globalisation

Countries trading with each other causes worldwide economic growth. So some organisations exist to push this.

1) World Trade Organisation (WTO) — sets rules to make trading fair. It promotes free trade, which means that no tariffs (taxes) are paid on imported goods. This helps poorer countries join in with trading.

2) World Bank — uses contributions from richer countries to give or lend money to poorer countries, to encourage them to trade. Money is also given to improve living standards and reduce world poverty.

3) International Monetary Fund (IMF) — manages world economies and tries to increase employment levels. A country needs to be a member of the IMF to be able to borrow money from the World Bank.

The UK is represented at these organisations by the Chancellor of the Exchequer and the Secretary of State for International Development. Representatives from each member country have a say, but it's the richer countries who tend to run the show because they put in more money. And if richer countries are making the decisions then they may well put their own trading interests before the needs of poorer countries.

Fair and Ethical Trade Help to Improve Life for Producers

Trading with countries helps their economic development. But producers in poor countries can end up being paid very little for their goods. This means extremely low wages and poor working conditions. That's where these initiatives come in...

Fair Trade	• Fair trade means producers in poor countries get a decent price for their goods. • Products are bought directly from producers to cut out the middleman, so producers get more money. • To display the FAIRTRADE Mark, companies must treat their workers fairly and respect the environment. This means doing things like paying decent wages, banning child labour and improving safety standards.

> Fair trade isn't without problems though. E.g. it can make life worse for farmers who aren't in the scheme.

Ethical Trade	• The Ethical Trading Initiative (ETI) works to improve the lives and working conditions of producers across the world by improving wages, health and safety and hours of work. • Companies that sign up to the ETI are responsible for making sure all their workers are well treated and have human rights, as many poorer countries don't have laws to protect their workers.

The World Bank — kinda like a polite Robin Hood then...

Basically, everyone knows it's really unfair that many people in poorer countries are living in poverty while people in richer countries use up loads of resources. So rich countries are trying to help out — but they still have their own agenda of making sure their own country's economy is OK. Talk about tough decisions...

Global Problems

I'd better take your mind off the economy... so here's a page about the really big problems in the world.

There are Loads of Problems Facing the Global Community

POPULATION GROWTH AND POVERTY ARE HUGE PROBLEMS

The world's population is rising rapidly, particularly in towns and cities in poorer countries.

- Overcrowding leads to more people living in slums. Many people have poor health because disease spreads easily in the crowded, unsanitary conditions and there's limited healthcare to treat disease.
- Much of the world's population live in poverty — they don't have enough money to buy food, so they become ill, can't work, and sink deeper into poverty — 30 000 children die each day due to poverty.
- Crime levels increase as people need to steal to survive.
- Population growth puts extra strain on the world's resources — see below...

WE'RE USING UP THE EARTH'S RESOURCES TOO FAST

This isn't sustainable — see page 27.

Natural resources include fossil fuels (coal, oil, gas), minerals (iron ore, copper), land and water.

- Many resources are running out because we're using them up much faster than they can be replaced.
- Demand for resources is increasing as living standards rise (e.g. we use more energy for air conditioners, etc.).
- There aren't enough resources to go round, so better-off people tend to end up with most of them. In fact, the richest 20% of the world's population consume 80% of the resources — shocking.
- Competition for scarce resources can lead to conflict and war.

  E.g. Angola, in Africa, had a 27-year-long civil war because different political groups wanted to take advantage of the rich diamond resources in the country. Many people fled the country as refugees.

Fuel Prices are Increasing...

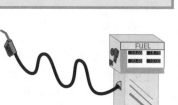

1) Demand for fossil fuels is soaring — partly because China and India have become more industrialised. This means that sellers can charge high prices.

2) Some countries rich in resources are politically unstable and prices rise when it gets risky getting fuel.
   E.g. petrol rose by about 2p per litre in 2002 when trouble escalated in the Middle East.

3) Burning fossil fuels causes climate change (see page 26). So in the UK, the amount of excise duty tax on petrol and diesel has been increased to encourage people to use less.

...Which Causes Problems for Poorer People and LEDCs

Higher fuel prices are annoying for those who can afford them — but they're a real problem for those who can't.

1) Most households in the UK need to spend a similar amount on fuel, so poorer households spend a larger proportion of their income on fuel than richer ones. Increases in fuel prices mean that poorer households mightn't have enough money left for other things and might have to choose between heating or eating, say.

2) Higher fuel prices mean higher food prices — it costs more to run farm machinery and to transport produce.

3) If LEDCs can't afford to buy fuel, their economic growth is limited. Food production is less efficient using hand-powered tools than using fuel-powered machinery, so more people will live in poverty.

4) Increased poverty can lead to a country borrowing more money and falling into a cycle of debt (see p. 22).

5) To make matters worse, when fossil fuel prices rise, MEDCs want more biofuels because they're cheaper. To make money from this, LEDCs grow more fuel crops and less food crops, meaning people go hungry.

It's all about supply and demand...

As if it wasn't enough that we're running out of resources, each of us is using more and there are more people in the world to provide for. So any way you look at it, there's not enough to go around and it can't carry on.

Supporting People in LEDCs

A big way that LEDCs (that's less economically developed countries, remember) can be given a helping hand is through international aid and debt relief. Different sorts of aid have their own advantages and disadvantages.

International Aid is Given from One Country to Another

1) Aid is given by one country to another in the form of money or resources (e.g. food, doctors).

2) The country that gives the aid, usually an MEDC, is called the donor — the one that gets the aid, usually an LEDC, is called the recipient.

See 22 for more on MEDCs and LEDCs.

3) There are two main sources of aid from donor countries — governments (paid for by taxes) and Non-Governmental Organisations (NGOs, paid for by voluntary donations).

4) There are two different ways donor governments can give aid to recipient countries:

   • Directly to the recipient — this is called bilateral aid. Sometimes this is tied — meaning it's given with the condition that the recipient country has to buy the goods and services it needs from the donor country.

   • Indirectly through an international organisation like the UN (see p. 62) or the World Bank (see p. 23). The international organisation distributes the aid — this is called multilateral aid.

5) Aid can be classed as either short-term or long-term depending on what it's used for:

Type of Aid	What it is	Advantage to recipient	Disadvantage to recipient
Short-term or humanitarian aid	Money or resources to help recipient countries cope with emergencies, e.g. earthquakes, wars.	The impact of the aid will be more immediate — more people will survive the emergency.	The development of a country remains unchanged. It may become reliant on aid.
Long-term or development aid	Money or resources to help recipient countries become more developed, e.g to improve healthcare.	Countries will be less reliant on foreign aid as they become more developed.	It can take a while before the aid benefits a country, e.g. hospitals take a long time to be built.
Debt relief	Some or all of a country's debt (see p. 22) is cancelled.	They can use money they make to develop rather than to pay back the debt.	Some people worry that it encourages irresponsible borrowing, or that the money will not go to help poor people.

6) Some recipient countries don't use aid effectively because they have corrupt governments — the government uses the money and resources to fund their lifestyle or to pay for political events.

NGOs and Governments Have Different Spending Priorities

1) The UK government's DFID (Department for International Development) spend billions of pounds each year. About 10% of their money goes on humanitarian aid, and the rest on development projects.

2) NGOs, e.g. charities, also spend money on humanitarian aid and development projects. In addition, they spend money acting as pressure groups to try to convince governments to do more to solve problems. E.g. Oxfam has criticised the US government for providing short-term rather than long-term aid to Ethiopia.

3) Here are examples of development projects that aid from governments and NGOs goes to fund:

   • Constructing schools to improve literacy rates, and hospitals to reduce death rates.
   • Building dams and wells to improve clean water supplies.
   • Providing farming knowledge and equipment to improve agriculture.

The DFID has to help countries meet the UN's Millennium Development Goals (see page 63).

4) The DFID also funds big projects in LEDCs that charities couldn't afford to pay for, e.g. supporting democratic elections, building roads and improving electricity supplies.

Bigger isn't always better...

Big, prestigious aid projects, such as large irrigation dams, sometimes break down because the villagers can't maintain them. Small-scale projects can be more successful — especially if local people can maintain them. For example, contour bunding (building small walls across slopes to stop water running off fields) has been successfully used to increase crop yields in dry areas of countries like Burkina Faso and India.

Climate Change

Environmental issues are a problem for everybody, and guess what... you need to know why.

Global Warming is a Long-Term Increase in Temperature

1) Global warming is the increase in the average temperature of the Earth's surface over the last century.

2) It's now generally agreed that it's largely caused by human activity — things like deforestation, farming and burning fossil fuels mean there are more greenhouses gases, like carbon dioxide, in the atmosphere.

3) Greenhouse gases trap heat from the Sun, which causes the Earth to heat up too much.

4) Global warming is causing ice caps to melt and sea levels to rise — many low-lying places may flood, displacing people and causing agricultural land to be lost.

Global Warming Leads to Climate Change

1) Climate change is a significant change in the weather of an area over a long period of time.

2) It's a massive problem:

- Changing rainfall patterns (more floods or droughts) disrupt agriculture, leading to food shortages.
- The competition for water could lead to war between some countries.
- Weather is getting more extreme — events like hurricanes kill people and destroy homes and livelihoods.

3) Coping with the effects of climate change costs a lot of money, e.g. building flood defences, rebuilding homes, supporting farmers unable to grow crops.

4) So it's really important that we stop the problem getting worse...

We Need to Reduce Carbon Dioxide Emissions

Burning fossil fuels releases a lot of carbon dioxide. We can reduce this by:

- using less energy, e.g. by cycling instead of driving, switching off lights, etc.
- getting energy from other sources, like solar power, wind power, wave power and tidal energy.

These energy sources don't give out carbon dioxide AND they're renewable — they'll never run out.

Renewable energy is sustainable because it allows people today to get what they need (energy) without stopping people in the future from getting what they need.

See the next page for more on sustainability.

International Efforts Aim to Combat Global Warming

Countries are working together to reduce emissions — because global warming affects everyone.

1) At the 1992 UN Earth Summit, world leaders recognised that there's a link between industrial activity and environmental damage, and that sustainable development is needed (see page 27).

2) Many countries signed up to the Kyoto Protocol in 1997. Developed countries agreed to reduce greenhouse gas emissions, monitor climate change and protect the environment.

3) But not all countries wanted to sign up — the USA and Australia believed that if they met the Kyoto targets it would significantly damage their economic growth.

They were also a bit peeved that poorer countries were 'let off' the targets, to allow them to develop.

4) The Gothenburg Protocol (2005) sets emissions targets for European countries and the USA — it aims to cut harmful gas emissions by 2010 to reduce pollution.

5) In 2007, leaders from the G8 nations (see p. 63) agreed to halve carbon dioxide emissions by 2050.

Combat global warming — have a HUGE snowball fight...

... which may not work, but it'd be fun to try. The problem yet again is money — reducing emissions means you can't produce as much, or you have to invest in expensive greener production methods. Ooops.

Environmental Problems and Sustainability

Like Ronaldo charging on towards the goal, here are some things that really need to be tackled.

Problems, Problems, Problems...

PROBLEM: Too much rubbish and not enough places to put it all.

To try to reduce the amount of rubbish that goes to landfill (big holes in the ground), many local councils have switched to fortnightly rubbish collections — general household waste is collected one week and recycling the next:

- This encourages people to sort their waste and recycle, so that less waste goes to landfill.
- But general waste left lying around poses a health risk to residents, especially in summer, because it's a source of food for rats, which can spread disease. So many residents aren't happy about fortnightly collections.

Councils have to pay landfill tax for every tonne of waste that goes to landfill. So the more they recycle, the more money they save.

PROBLEM: Too much traffic on the roads.

Different transport policies have been introduced to try to reduce traffic on the roads, which will also help to reduce pollution and global warming.

- Congestion charges aim to reduce traffic and encourage public transport use by charging people to drive in congested areas, e.g. central London.
- The government and local councils spend money on improving public transport, creating cycle paths and making footpaths safer for pedestrians — all to encourage people to reduce their car use.

Alternative fuel cars, e.g. hydrogen fuel cells or biodiesel, tend to do less damage to the environment than petrol or diesel cars. So congestion charges don't apply to them to encourage more people to drive them.

Traffic Jam

PROBLEM: Businesses use loads of energy and create lots of waste, which is bad for the environment.

Businesses can reduce their impact on the environment (and save money) by:

- Switching off computers and lights at night to reduce the amount of wasted energy.
- Reducing, reusing and recycling materials to reduce waste, or using sustainable materials.
- Encouraging workers to car share or work from home to reduce the number of cars on the road.

There are packaging regulations which demand businesses pay towards recycling their packaging.

Sustainable Development means Thinking of the Future

Sustainable development is about improving quality of life for people now, but in a way that can continue into the future. Oooh, it makes me feel all warm inside...

For development to be sustainable, we all need to change our behaviour and use resources in a way that can be kept going for a long time without causing harm to people or the environment. For example:

1) You can reduce energy use, e.g. by insulating your home and using energy-efficient light bulbs.
2) Businesses can use less packaging and invest in sustainable technologies.
   E.g. technologies that use renewable energy sources, like solar panels.
3) Organisations can educate people about reducing energy consumption and provide encouragement.
   E.g. the Energy Saving Trust gives free advice for people wanting to save energy.
4) The government can invest in energy-efficient technologies and provide incentives for reducing energy use.
   E.g. giving people with old, inefficient boilers money towards a new one.

We all need to act NOW...

... well, maybe just finish reading this page before you go on a mad dash to change all your light bulbs to energy-savers. But I have to be off, I've swapped my car for a bike and I live a long way away... wish me luck...

Tackling Environmental Problems

At least people are doing something about these problems — and the more people work together, the better.

The Rio Earth Summit Introduced Agenda 21

1) The 1992 UN Earth Summit led to an agreement that action should be taken to protect the environment and deal with world poverty.

2) More than 170 governments signed up to an agreement called Agenda 21.

3) Agenda 21 outlines actions that can be taken at local, national and international levels to combat poverty, hunger, war and environmental destruction.

Well, I think we should protect the environment and deal with world poverty.

Oh, okay then. Why not?

There's also Local Agenda 21 — see the next page.

Environmental Groups Campaign for Greener Solutions

1) Environmental groups try to stop people harming the planet, e.g. through pollution or deforestation. They try to introduce environmentally responsible solutions instead.

2) They do this by investigating any abuse of the environment and developing campaigns to raise awareness about what's happening and who's doing it. Then they encourage the public to support their campaigns, e.g. by joining demonstrations, writing to their local MP or donating money to help fund campaigns.

3) This puts pressure on the people responsible to change their ways and stop damaging the environment. E.g.

> Greenpeace helped reduce deforestation in the Amazon by putting pressure on the biggest cattle companies to change their ways and commit to "zero deforestation in their supply chains".

> Friends of the Earth campaign for carbon emissions to be cut. E.g. by encouraging people to sign a petition to get the government to give local councils more money towards cutting carbon emissions.

Different Scales of Action can Really Make a Difference

1) The world's oceans are polluted with harmful chemicals from oil tankers, other ships and dumped waste.

2) Adding to this, land pollution can be washed into the sea, e.g. fuel spills, fertilisers and factory waste.

3) This marine pollution harms wildlife and their habitats, and can damage our health if it gets into the food chain, e.g. by contaminating fish which is then caught for human food.

4) Most countries have rules about dumping waste materials at sea. But marine pollution is difficult to control because pollution spreads over international boundaries — so countries need to work together:

- The London Convention (1972) was one of the first global agreements to not dump waste into the sea.
- The International Maritime Organisation (IMO) regulates international shipping and environmental concerns. E.g. the IMO has phased out the largest and oldest oil tankers to reduce spillages.
- The UK government's Marine and Coastal Access Act includes plans to create Marine Conservation Zones that are protected from any damaging activities.
- Businesses like shipping companies and factories get heavy fines if they don't follow strict regulations.
- Farmers follow the Nitrate Pollution Regulations to reduce nitrate pollution from fertilisers they use.
- We can all do our bit, e.g. by not dropping litter, disposing of waste correctly (don't just flush stuff down the loo), using fewer plastic bags and buying products from environmentally responsible suppliers.

> ## It's up to you... and you... and you... and you... and you... and you... and you... and you...
> It's much easier to solve problems when everyone works together and does what's in their power to help. You mightn't have enough clout to give polluting countries a good telling off, but you can turn your light off.

Individual and Local Action

Even though the problems described in this section sound enormous, everyone's contributions count, whether you're volunteering, helping a charity or recycling bottles. As someone once said, it's nice to be nice.

Local Councils *have Developed* Local Action Plans

1) Part of Agenda 21 (see previous page) is Local Agenda 21, which has the slogan 'Think globally, act locally'.
2) Every local council is encouraged to develop a local action plan to look at ways of conserving energy, recycling, reducing pollution and protecting the countryside.
3) As well as council action, Local Agenda 21 stresses the importance of the individual.
4) 'Think globally, act locally' encourages everyone to consider the environment and do their bit to work towards sustainable development. This could include using the car less, planting trees, buying local goods, recycling more, etc.
5) Local Agenda 21 helps to increase community participation, reduce energy bills, reduce waste and create a cleaner environment.

Individuals and Communities are Interdependent

1) People within communities are interdependent — everyone is affected by the things other people do.
2) There are loads of ways that individuals can help improve their community on page 14.
3) Communities also affect each other — most of the world's population is interdependent because:
   - We trade with each other — loads of the things we buy come from other regions or countries.
   - Many businesses we work for and buy from are nationwide or multinational (e.g. McDonald's).
4) Many charities, e.g. Children in Need or the Royal National Institute of Blind People, work at a national level. They help people all over the UK, and are often more successful at fund-raising than local charities because they have more resources. E.g. Children in Need has an annual 'Telethon' which raises millions of pounds.
5) There are also charities and other organisations that work internationally...

Individuals *Can Help* Solve International Problems

Supporting international charities is a way to help communities across the world. You can help by:

VOLUNTEERING:

E.g. PLATFORM2 is a volunteer programme funded by the UK's Department for International Development.

- It pays for young people to fly overseas to volunteer in countries like India, Kenya or Peru.
- The volunteers might help build things like hand water pumps or play areas, teach in schools or raise awareness of HIV/AIDS.
- Afterwards, they're expected to tell people in their communities about the work they did. This increases awareness of the problems.

The water pump was much easier to use when the tiny horse sat on top of it.

RAISING OR DONATING MONEY:

Charities like Oxfam and Comic Relief help tackle poverty in poorer countries. Individuals can help by:
- donating money, e.g. for farming tools or for mosquito nets to prevent the spread of malaria.
- taking part in fund-raising activities, e.g. sponsored bathing in baked beans.

I keep recycling jokes, but no one seems to be impressed...

OK, so this is a mildly cheesy page about generally being nice and a good citizen. But, cringeworthy or not, getting involved in local issues can give you a great feeling of satisfaction as well as improving the world.

Quick Test

This section's all about becoming globally aware. There are lots of really complicated issues here, and no easy solutions. The questions below should make sure you've got a grip on the facts — what you choose to do with the facts is up to you. Try to answer each question, and if you can't, just look back for the answer in the section (they're all there somewhere, promise). Congratulations — you are now globally aware.

1) What is meant by the term 'public sector'? Give an example of a public sector job.
2) What is meant by the term 'private sector'? Give an example of a private sector job.
3) How can private businesses be good for local economies?
4) Suggest how the government can help the country's economy to grow.
5) Name one factor that can cause economic uncertainty.
6) What is a 'direct tax'? Give three examples of direct taxes.
7) What is an 'indirect tax'? Give three examples of indirect taxes.
8) Name three important services that taxes are spent on.
9) What type of tax pays for local services like rubbish collections?
10) What is the role of the Chancellor of the Exchequer in the government?
11) What are LEDCs and MEDCs?
12) Why are international debts an increasing problem for many LEDCs?
13) What is globalisation? Explain why it has increased.
14) Why do multinational companies often have their factories in poor countries?
15) Give two good effects and two bad effects of increasing globalisation.
16) Name three organisations which promote globalisation.
17) What do companies have to do if they want to display the Fair Trade logo?
18) Is the world's population increasing, decreasing, or staying about the same?
19) What are the main effects of overcrowding and poverty?
20) Why are fuel prices increasing? What problems does this cause in (a) MEDCs, and (b) LEDCs?
21) What is international aid?
22) What's an NGO? Where do they get their money from?
23) What is the difference between bilateral and multilateral aid?
24) Give an advantage and a drawback of (a) humanitarian aid, (b) development aid, and (c) debt relief.
25) What problem has led to some governments not using aid effectively?
26) Give a couple of examples of development projects that are funded by aid.
27) What is causing global warming? What problems is it likely to lead to? How can it be stopped?
28) What is the Kyoto Protocol?
29) What is sustainable development?
30) What is the aim of Agenda 21?
31) How does the ocean become polluted? Why is it especially difficult for governments to deal with?
32) Give an example of how marine pollution has been reduced due to action by:
    a) the UK government,
    b) international organisations.
33) Give two ways that individuals can support international charities.

Being British

It's <u>hard</u> to say what <u>Britishness</u> is all about in a short, snappy sentence. So I've used a whole page.

Being British <u>**involves**</u> <u>Cultural Traditions</u> <u>**and**</u> <u>Shared Values</u>

People from many <u>different cultures</u> live in Britain, so 'being British' is pretty <u>tough to define</u>.
Basically, it means having a sense of <u>belonging</u> to <u>British society</u>, e.g. joining in with traditions:

- Britain's <u>cultural traditions</u> include more than wearing bowler hats and drinking afternoon tea, you know.
- <u>Trooping the Colour</u>, the <u>Queen's Speech</u> and <u>Royal Ascot</u> (a famous horse racing event) are all very British.
- Parliament has loads of traditions, like <u>MPs say 'aye' or 'no'</u> when voting. It's tradition to set <u>Guy Fawkes</u> alight on <u>Bonfire Night</u>, dance around a <u>maypole</u> on <u>May Day</u> and stuff yourself silly on <u>Pancake Day</u>.

Certain <u>values</u> are also important for the <u>British way of life</u>:

① Personal freedom as a basic right

- Personal freedom means being <u>free</u> to make your <u>own</u> <u>choices</u> and <u>decisions</u>. You can choose your own career (within reason), how to spend your leisure time, how to dress, etc.
- But this freedom has to be <u>controlled with rules</u> so that <u>other people's rights</u> aren't reduced by your choices. E.g. some shopping centres have banned people from wearing <u>hoodies</u>, to try to reduce <u>intimidating</u> behaviour.

Rather.

The Union Jack and the British Bulldog are patriotic symbols of Britain.

② Tolerating and respecting diversity

- Britain is a <u>multicultural</u> society so there's a lot of <u>diversity</u>.
- Being British is about <u>tolerating diversity</u>, <u>respecting the freedoms of others</u>, and not discriminating against people who are different. E.g. people have the right to choose what they eat, how they worship, etc.

③ Equal opportunities for all

- Being British is about believing that <u>everyone</u> has an <u>equal chance</u> in life. E.g. which person gets a job should depend on their <u>skills</u> and abilities, rather than things like race, religion, sex or age.
- People have fought for many years for <u>equality</u>, e.g. equal rights for <u>women</u>, <u>gay rights</u>, etc.
- People and companies can be taken to <u>court</u> if they <u>discriminate</u>, e.g. it's <u>illegal</u> to <u>pay men more than women</u> who do the same job.

④ Representative democracy

- <u>Democracy</u> gives almost every adult the <u>right</u> to have a <u>say</u> in how Britain is run.
- We don't get a say in every single decision — that'd take ages. Instead, people <u>elect</u> the Members of Parliament (MPs) and local councillors whose polices they agree with the most, so that their <u>views are represented</u> in Parliament and in the town hall. This is called <u>representative democracy</u>.
- The British Parliament has been <u>copied</u> all over the world as it's thought to be one of the <u>fairest</u> ways to run a country.

See pages 47-53 for more on democracy.

⑤ British laws

- Laws are created to make life <u>fair</u> — <u>everyone</u> in Britain must follow the <u>same set of rules</u>
- So illegal acts <u>won't be tolerated</u>, even if they're legal in other countries, e.g. <u>forced marriages</u>.
- Laws also protect our <u>health and safety</u> and our <u>rights</u>.

See pages 36-40 for more on laws.

The <u>UK</u> <u>**is Made Up of**</u> <u>England, Scotland, Wales</u> <u>**and**</u> <u>Northern Ireland</u>

1) England, Scotland, Wales and Northern Ireland gradually became <u>united</u> through history to form a powerful <u>United Kingdom</u> (UK).

Britain = England, Scotland and Wales.
UK = Britain and Northern Ireland.

2) But England was always the <u>dominant</u> country. In recent times the Welsh, Scottish and Irish have fought to gain <u>more control</u> of their own countries. Some government decisions are now taken by the <u>National Assembly for Wales</u>, the <u>Scottish Parliament</u> and the <u>Northern Ireland Assembly</u>. The passing of powers from central to regional government is called <u>devolution</u> — see page 53.

3) Eventually, each country within the UK may choose to become <u>independent</u> — but only if they can be <u>powerful</u> enough on their own, e.g. if they can support their own <u>economy</u>.

Being British — *1. Complain about the weather 2. Queue for the Post Office 3. Put the kettle on*

There are some things about being British that are easy to define — usually it's the silly things or our worst traits. But trying to say what we're like as a <u>culture</u> is a toughy. So <u>learn</u> this page and it'll be much <u>easier</u>.

Cultural Diversity — Origins

Cultural diversity just means the variety of people and backgrounds in an area.

Centuries of Migration has Helped to Shape the UK's Community...

1) People have been coming to live here for centuries. Must be those long, hot summers we get.

2) Romans, Normans, Saxons, Vikings, Celts, Picts — everyone who's invaded Britain over the years has brought a bit of their culture with them, from sport to art to religion.

3) In Tudor times, many Protestants came to England from Catholic Europe to escape persecution for their religious beliefs.

4) Later, many Irish Catholics came to Britain as economic migrants, to escape poverty and food shortages.

5) Many Jews were persecuted in Nazi Germany in the 1930s and came to Britain as political migrants.

6) After World War II, the government encouraged people from the Commonwealth (see page 61) to come and work here, to help the British economy to recover.

7) Many people from Pakistan, Bangladesh, China and India came to live in Britain in the 1940s and 50s, for a better life.

- Economic migrants — people who move somewhere with more job opportunities, to earn more money for a better life.
- Political migrants — people who move to get away from persecution, e.g. being threatened because of their political or religious beliefs.
- Refugees — people escaping problems in their own countries, e.g. war, and who are unable or afraid to return.
- Asylum seekers — refugees trying to get given the right to stay in a host country.
- Illegal immigrants — people who arrive illegally and claim asylum but aren't refugees.

... and it's Still Changing Today

1) Communities change as people continue to move here from different places and as people move away too.

2) Centuries ago, people didn't really travel much outside their home area. But now with improved transport, including air travel, more and more people have the opportunity to live and work in different places.

3) People in the European Union (EU) can live and work in any other EU country, so migration is easy. People can choose to be temporary migrants and stay for as long as they want.

4) Many asylum seekers and refugees come to the UK to escape wars in Iraq, Iran and Afghanistan. One reason why people tend to come here is because we have fewer immigration restrictions than many other countries.

5) Despite all these comings and goings, different regions of the UK still have different cultural identities, depending on the history of the area (e.g. Selby was a coal-mining town), people's accents (e.g. Geordies), jobs available (e.g. Padstow is a fishing village), historical rivalries (e.g. Lancashire and Yorkshire) or tourism (e.g. Blackpool).

Different People Bring Different Skills and Ideas to the Community

The UK's economy, sports and entertainment have been influenced by different people over the years, e.g:

- French businessmen brought their trading knowledge in the 13th century and started London's financial services.
- Gurkha soldiers from Nepal have been part of the British Army for almost 200 years.
- Irish labourers were an essential part of the British workforce in the 1950s and 60s, building motorways and railways.
- Many Pakistanis came to Britain in the 1960s as qualified doctors and worked for the NHS.
- Many Polish immigrants have worked in the construction industry since Poland joined the EU in 2004.

- Mohamed Al-Fayed is a multi-millionaire Egyptian businessman who owns Harrods in London, one of the largest department stores in the world and a big tourist attraction.
- Amir Khan is a British-Pakistani boxer and Britain's youngest Olympic boxing medallist.
- 'Slumdog Millionaire' is a smash-hit British film starring Bollywood actors from India.

Variety is the spice of life, an' all that...

Multiculturalism makes life more varied. It's not a new thing either — it's been around for centuries.

Cultural Diversity

Understanding the differences between people and how they live can broaden your mind. And be quite fun too.

The UK has Diverse Ethnic and Religious Cultures...

1) The UK is multicultural, which means it's made up of many different cultures. Most towns and cities are cosmopolitan — they're made up of people and cultures from around the world.

2) Different cultures bring different traditions, faiths, food, music and much more.

3) It makes a country more interesting, with diverse cultural influences and festivals, e.g. Chinese New Year, Diwali (Festival of Light). The Notting Hill Carnival is a hugely popular street party that celebrates multicultural Britain each year.

4) Experiencing other cultures helps people to understand and respect differences.

... But Everyone has Their Own Social Identity

1) But because the UK has such a cultural diversity, it can be hard to have a sense of identity of your own.

> E.g. if you were born in Wales but now live in Scotland, have a Russian mum and an Indian dad... then what kind of traditions would you follow? What would be your first language? What would your faith be?

2) Social identity is about which groups in society you relate to and feel part of, and which you don't.

3) You might relate to lots of different groups, so have multiple social identities.

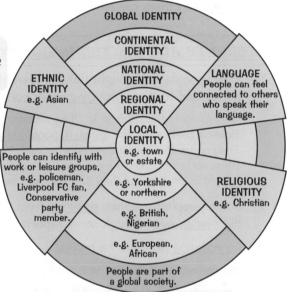

Differences of identity

- Some people identify very strongly with one particular group. Different groups living side by side can cause tension, e.g. religious tension in Northern Ireland, fights between rival football fans.
- It takes tolerance to live peacefully and accept other people's differences (see next page for more).

Cohesive Communities Bring Together People with Different Identities

1) When the whole of society works together for a common cause it encourages integration, respect and a better understanding between communities. This is called community cohesion.

2) There are lots of ways of promoting community cohesion:

For example:

1) Language classes are provided for people who don't speak English, and children in British schools are taught in English, so that we have a common language and mutual understanding. People are more likely to integrate if they don't have language difficulties.

2) Foreigners wanting to become British citizens must pass a 'Life in the UK' test, so that they know about British culture and can speak English. This is meant to encourage integration and gives a sense of national identity.

3) Local councils have things like allotment projects to bring together people from different communities.

4) Some schools and towns are twinned with other places, to improve knowledge of other cultures.

5) Students are educated about cultural diversity.
(I know it's literally staring you in the face, but it's an easy point to forget.)

So it's not just spies who have multiple identities...

Some people think there should be a new national holiday to celebrate being British, because it'd help bring the country together in a sense of national identity. Either that, or they just want an extra day's holiday.

Discrimination and Disadvantage

Britain is full of diverse cultures and communities. Part of being British is to tolerate and respect differences between people (see British values on p. 31). After all, life would be pretty boring if everyone were the same.

Not Everyone is Tolerant of People who are Different

Cultural diversity's great if people have mutual respect. But this isn't always the case...

1) Some people are prejudiced — they think badly of other people without good reason for doing so. It's often because of stereotypes — commonly held beliefs about groups of people. It may be based on skin colour, culture, religion, nationality, sexual orientation, weight, age or hair colour.

2) Some people treat certain people unfairly because of their prejudices. This is discrimination.

3) Discrimination can be direct, e.g. verbally abusing a member of a particular group, or indirect — making rules that disadvantage one group, e.g. not allowing employees to wear anything on their heads discriminates against Sikh men.

Intolerance of others can lead to racial tensions and violence, e.g. the 2001 'race riots' in Bradford and Oldham.

Prejudice and Discrimination come from a Lack of Understanding

1) Many people are brought up with stereotypical ideas about people, and it's hard to change these. It can lead to them resenting other cultures.

   Some people think Britain is "their country", so other cultures shouldn't be allowed to live and work here. Political parties like the British National Party (BNP) and the British National Front support these views. They argue that immigrants take houses, jobs and benefits that are meant for British people, so it's unfair. However, many people from ethnic minorities work long hours for low pay. They tend to be the poorest people in society and they do jobs that many other people wouldn't take.

2) Some people form their opinions from what they see in the media, even though some reports might be biased.

   Some people stereotype all British Muslims as extremists since the London bombings in 2005.

3) Acceptance needs to be mutual — some people think that other cultures don't integrate into society.

   Immigrants often choose to live with a group of people from a similar background because it makes adjusting to life in a new country much easier — neighbours will speak their first language, share their faith and understand their culture. But this can lead to 'ethnic ghettos' — areas of mainly one ethnic group who become socially excluded.

The Government aims to Educate People and Promote Equality

1) Anti-discrimination laws make it illegal to discriminate, e.g. against women (Sex Discrimination Act 1975), ethnic minorities (Race Relations Act 1976) or people with disabilities (Disability Discrimination Act 1975).

2) The Equalities and Human Rights Commission looks into any unfair goings-on, such as social housing being provided for immigrants before other people on the waiting list. It advises the government on equality.

3) The government provides training grants and loans to help disadvantaged people improve their educational level, attend training courses and access higher education.

4) Many hospitals have translators, and councils provide leaflets in other languages so that everyone can access public services.

5) The "Let's Kick Racism Out of Football" campaign works to challenge discrimination in sport.

6) Child poverty, regardless of race or religion, is one of the big inequalities that needs to be tackled. The government are trying to address this through their 'Every Child Matters' programme of change, e.g. by reforming the benefits system for families.

R-E-S-P-E-C-T — what you need for e-qual-i-ty...

Educating people about cultural diversity, encouraging communities to integrate and promoting equality can help to wipe out discrimination. Everyone should feel like they belong and should be treated fairly. Ho hum.

Quick Test

What ho, it's the end of the section already — better see if you've taken it all in old chap.

It's only four pages, but there are lots of ideas crammed in, so have another read over them if you need to.

Then, get yourself a nice cuppa in the British way, settle down and see how many of these questions you can answer correctly. You may already have your own opinions about life in Britain, but it's always good to know what other people think.

1) Describe what 'being British' means.
2) Give three royal traditions that are associated with Britain.
3) Give two other British cultural traditions.
4) What does 'personal freedom' mean?
5) Why do there need to be limits to personal freedom?
6) Give an example of how British values respect diversity.
7) Give an example of illegal discrimination in the workplace.
8) What is meant by 'representative democracy'?
9) Give two reasons why we have laws in Britain.
10) What's the difference between the UK and Great Britain?
11) What is meant by the term 'devolution'?
12) Who makes some of the government decisions in Wales?
13) What might stop a country like Wales from becoming independent from the UK?
14) What are whales? a) fish
                        b) mammals
                        c) insects
15) What are economic migrants?
16) Give an example of a group of political migrants who came to live in Britain in the 20th century.
17) Define the following terms: a) refugee
                                 b) asylum seeker
                                 c) illegal immigrant
18) Give one reason why it's easier to migrate from the UK to another European country now than it was centuries ago.
19) Give two reasons why different regions have different cultural identities.
20) Give two examples of how the economy has been influenced by immigration.
21) What does the term 'multicultural' mean?
22) Give two ways in which multiculturalism is good for Britain.
23) Define these terms: a) social identity
                         b) interdependence
                         c) community cohesion
24) Give an example of one thing the British government does to encourage community cohesion.
25) What does it mean if someone is prejudiced?
26) What is discrimination?
27) Give one reason why some people think that immigrants shouldn't be allowed to work in Britain.
28) Give one reason why other people think that immigrants should be allowed to work in Britain.
29) Why might immigrants choose to live with people of a similar background?
30) What is an 'ethnic ghetto' and why do they exist?
31) Give an example of an anti-discrimination law in Britain.

Laws — What They Are

Laws stop us doing exactly what we want, which sounds bad at first, but if you ever read Lord of the Flies, you might start thinking that's a good thing...

Being Lord of the Flies is a thankless task...

Laws are About Rules

1) If you want one (long) <u>definition of law</u> then this should do:

> "Law is a formal method of controlling people and society through rules set down and then enforced through courts and the legal system."

2) British laws are intended to make life <u>fair</u>, so we're all judged by the same set of rules. <u>Everyone</u> in a country should follow the same laws — even the people who make them.

3) Every time someone <u>breaks a law</u> they are committing a <u>crime</u>.

Laws Help Society Run Smoothly and Safely

1) Laws are there for people's <u>health</u> and <u>safety</u>. They're supposed to protect us, and stop us doing things that might be <u>harmful</u> or <u>dangerous</u>. For example:

   • The ban on <u>smoking in public places</u> was brought in to protect the health of non-smokers from poisonous chemicals from cigarettes, and to encourage smokers to quit.

   • <u>Drink-driving laws</u> aim to make things safer for all road users.

Ethel agreed that lawns helped things run smoothly.

2) Laws help <u>enforce order</u> — if people could do whatever they wanted there would be complete chaos and society would eventually break down (this is called <u>anarchy</u> — think of a load of young kids shut in a house with no adults for a week and you'll get the general idea...). Society only works properly if it has a <u>framework</u> to tell us what is and isn't acceptable behaviour.

Laws Protect People's Rights

1) Laws should <u>protect people's rights</u>. If any of our rights are threatened or ignored then the law should step in to <u>defend</u> them.

2) Criminal activity often infringes <u>human rights</u>, e.g. murder definitely infringes a person's <u>right to life</u>, and theft would infringe someone's <u>right to own property</u> and not have it taken away without good cause. Legal rights and consumer rights, etc. can also be threatened by illegal activity.

3) Some people talk about '<u>victimless crimes</u>', but they're quite hard to find — in most cases there will be victims, even if it's just the shareholders of a big company.

> E.g. some say <u>shoplifting</u> doesn't harm anyone — it's only stealing from companies and doesn't harm individuals. Others argue any stealing is wrong. There are also <u>knock-on effects</u> like damaging profits which might mean fewer jobs, or the shop covering the cost of stealing by raising its prices, leading to higher costs for everyone.

Laws Can Resolve Conflict

1) Sometimes people <u>can't agree</u> on something, but there's no obvious right and wrong in the situation.

2) For example — if someone allows their hedge to grow <u>really tall</u>, it might block light to their neighbour's house. It's <u>their</u> hedge, so you might argue that it's up to them how tall it grows. But is it really fair that their neighbour has to sit in the dark?

3) To try to make life fairer for everyone, <u>laws</u> about such matters are introduced and used to <u>resolve future conflicts</u>.

Disputes like this are settled in Civil Courts (see page 39).

Cole's Law — there to protect the public from dull salads...

The law affects nearly everything we do. It's the reason you can't drive a car or buy alcohol when you're 16. Laws are being <u>changed</u> all the time — old ones are scrapped and new ones introduced. E.g. it's now illegal to sell the most energy-inefficient lightbulbs. This law's meant to protect the environment (and ultimately us).

Making Laws

Laws aren't made up willy-nilly. There's a long process to <u>try</u> to make sure that they'll actually improve things.

A <u>Bill</u> is a <u>Rough Draft</u> of a Law

1) The <u>government</u> often changes the law — sometimes because they promised they would if they were elected, and sometimes because the public are putting <u>pressure</u> on them to do so.

2) The government does this by introducing a <u>Bill</u> to <u>Parliament</u>. A Bill has to pass through lots of stages and is <u>voted</u> on by MPs who have been elected by the public — it's all part of being a <u>democracy</u>.

3) Here are the <u>stages</u> in the process:

> Individual MPs can introduce Bills to Parliament too — these are called Private Members' Bills. They rarely get as far as to be made law though.

The Government draws up a Bill
The politicians don't just write the first thing that comes into their heads — they talk to <u>experts</u> on the topic of the new law and write out several drafts (usually a Green Paper, then a White Paper).

> Members of the public can also write to their MP or the government with their opinions on the proposed law.

The First Reading
This is just a formality really — the <u>title</u> of the Bill is read out in the House of Commons and a <u>date set</u> for the Second Reading.

The Second Reading
The general principles of the Bill are <u>debated</u> and a <u>vote</u> is taken — again this is in the House of Commons. If the Bill is voted against, it won't get through to the next stage.

Committee Stage
This is when each detail of the Bill is <u>scrutinised</u> and <u>voted</u> on. It's usually done by a group of 16-50 MPs. They often make <u>changes</u> to parts of the Bill.

Report Stage and Third Reading
The Committee <u>reports</u> to the House of Commons on which bits of the Bill it has changed. Then the Bill is read out again. It's debated and a vote is taken again.

> This gives politicians who weren't in the Committee a chance to get their two-pennies' worth in.

> And then this process happens <u>all over again</u> in the <u>House of Lords...</u>

> It can happen the other way round — through the House of Lords <u>first</u>, and <u>then</u> through the House of Commons.

...And then it goes back to the House of Commons
If the Lords make any changes, these have to be <u>agreed</u> by the House of Commons. The Bill will only become law when <u>both houses</u> agree on the exact wording. BUT — the Lords can only delay a Bill by a year. After that, the House of Commons can use the <u>Parliament Act</u> to override the House of Lords (and they do occasionally).

> The Bill can go back and forth loads of times. The official jargon for this is 'Ping Pong'.

Royal Assent
The Queen now 'signs off' the Bill. (Well, this is just a formality nowadays, and she doesn't really sign anything. The Royal Assent's just an <u>announcement</u> made in both Houses.)

It's now an Act of Parliament
It becomes <u>law</u> on a certain date.

<u>Judges</u> and the <u>European Union</u> Give Us Laws Too

1) All the decisions made by judges for the last 900 or so years have been written down — they've formed what's known as '<u>Common Law</u>'.

2) When cases come up in court today, judges consider <u>similar cases</u> and follow the decisions made in them.
However, if it's not something that's ever come up before, or if it's decided that the previous judgement is now too out of date, then a new decision is made — this becomes new Common Law.

3) <u>European law</u> comes <u>above</u> any other kind of law in Britain — no law can be passed if it conflicts with it.

You can become a fan of Parliament on Facebook — yes, really...
The Queen or King *can* say, "No, I don't like that law. You're not having it." — but the last one to do this was Queen Anne around 1707. In fact, the last time a monarch personally signed the Royal Assent was in 1854.

Conflicting Rights

Section One talked about how everyone has <u>rights</u>, but they sometimes <u>conflict</u> and must be compromised. Well, there are laws in place to sort out common conflicts, and that's what this page is about...

A <u>Conflict</u> of <u>Rights</u> <u>can be Resolved by</u> <u>Law</u>

In an <u>ideal world</u>, everyone would be granted all their rights, all the time. But rights aren't always straightforward — sometimes they <u>compete</u> and <u>conflict</u>.

See p. 6 for more on conflicting rights.

When a conflict of rights happens, the <u>law</u> is used to resolve issues <u>fairly</u>:

- An individual's rights can be restricted to <u>prevent a crime</u> or to <u>protect the rights of others</u>.
- A person's rights can be restricted as a <u>precaution</u>, to protect others from potential harm.
- The law puts the rights of the many — <u>the community</u> — <u>before</u> the rights of an individual.

EXAMPLE — children's rights

<u>Parents</u> have the <u>right</u> to bring up their own children. But any <u>abuse</u> or <u>neglect</u> is a breach of <u>children's rights</u>.

So the law allows local authorities to <u>restrict</u> parents' rights and take a child away if they're in physical or emotional <u>danger</u>. But this is a difficult decision for authorities to make — they've been accused of acting unjustly in some cases and not quickly enough in others.

EXAMPLE — suspects' rights

Everyone has the right to be considered <u>innocent</u> until proven <u>guilty</u>. But if someone's suspected of a <u>dangerous crime</u> they can be <u>held</u> until their case goes to court, even though they've not been found guilty yet. This <u>restricts</u> the suspect's rights but <u>protects</u> the community from potential danger.

EXAMPLE — road safety

Road safety laws are there to <u>prevent accidents</u> and <u>protect</u> road users — but to do this, they have to <u>restrict</u> some people's freedom, e.g. driving age restrictions, speed restrictions, drink-driving laws.

EXAMPLE — dangerous animals

The <u>Dangerous Wild Animals Act 1976</u> restricts people from owning a dangerous wild animal unless it presents <u>no risk</u> to the public, can be looked after correctly and the person has a licence.

The <u>Dangerous Dogs Act 1991</u> restricts people from <u>breeding</u> or <u>selling</u> certain types of dog to <u>protect</u> the rights of the public. This is because certain breeds, e.g. <u>pitbulls</u>, are prone to viciousness and have killed young children in the past.

Felix felt that there should be a clause in the Not-So-Dangerous Dogs Act about being made to wear silly hats.

EXAMPLE — anti-terrorism laws

Sometimes we're expected to <u>give up</u> some of our rights to try to <u>prevent terrorist attacks</u>. But there's a <u>fine balance</u> to be struck between <u>national security</u> and <u>upholding citizens' rights</u>.

- The <u>Prevention of Terrorism Act 2005</u> allows the government to <u>restrict</u> what <u>suspected terrorists</u> can do even if there's not enough <u>evidence</u> to charge them. The suspect's <u>mobile phone</u> and <u>internet</u> use can be restricted, or they can be put under <u>house arrest</u> or be banned from <u>certain places</u> (e.g. airports).
- But the law allowing police to <u>stop and search</u> random members of the public has been ruled <u>illegal</u> by the <u>European Court of Human Rights</u> because it breaches the public's right to <u>respect for their privacy</u>.
- Terror suspects can now be held <u>without charge</u> for up to <u>28 days</u>. Some people argue this is a <u>breach of human rights</u>, but others feel that we should do <u>whatever it takes</u> to fight terrorism.

Balancing rights — harder than walking a tightrope over Niagara Falls...

Human rights laws are there to <u>protect</u> our freedom, but some people think they protect the <u>wrong people</u>, like <u>terrorists</u>. When rights <u>conflict</u>, there has to be a <u>compromise</u> — so not everyone's going to be <u>happy</u>.

Civil Law

Civil law tends to be the <u>less dramatic</u> side of law — but you need to know about it anyway.

There are <u>Two Main Types of Law</u> — <u>Civil</u> and <u>Criminal</u>

Civil Law	Criminal Law
• Tries to <u>solve disputes</u> which may be between individuals, businesses or organisations.	• Attempts to <u>maintain law and order</u> and to protect citizens.
• Civil law includes <u>Family Law</u>, <u>Employment Law</u>, <u>Contract Law</u> (see below) and <u>ASBOs</u> (see the next page).	• Cases are normally started by the <u>police</u> through the <u>Crown Prosecution Service</u>.
• The court usually decides that the person/organisation in the wrong must pay <u>damages</u> or <u>compensation</u> to the other party (a money award).	• Criminal cases include theft, murder and drink-driving.
• Sometimes, one party might be <u>ordered</u> to do something, e.g. chop down a tree that is blocking a neighbour's light.	• Criminal cases may end in some sort of <u>punishment</u>, e.g. fines, probation, curfews or prison.

Civil Cases are Dealt with by <u>Magistrates</u> or <u>Courts</u>

1) Most civil cases <u>never</u> actually get to court — the people involved usually reach an agreement before then. Those that do get to court are most commonly heard in <u>County</u> or <u>High Courts</u>. However, some are heard by <u>magistrates</u>.

This is different from criminal cases, which almost all begin in the <u>magistrates' court</u>. There's more on criminal cases on p. 43.

2) The person starting a civil case is called the <u>claimant</u>.

3) The decision in civil cases is usually made by a <u>judge</u> or a <u>panel of judges</u> rather than a jury.

Family Matters are Dealt with by Civil Law...

1) When a couple get <u>divorced</u>, there are loads of things they need to sort out — like who the kids will live with, who'll get to keep the house, and how the money will be divided up (even who gets the dog).

2) The couple are encouraged to sort everything out <u>between themselves</u>, maybe with the help of a <u>mediator</u>. But if they <u>can't agree</u>, the <u>courts</u> will decide what will happen.

3) <u>Adoptions</u> are also dealt with by civil law. When a child is adopted, he or she becomes a <u>full member</u> of the new family, and has at least one new parent. The birth parents will have no more rights over the child.

4) <u>Courts</u> have to be satisfied that the child <u>can</u> be adopted (e.g. the birth parents have agreed), and that the person wanting to adopt the child will give the child a good home.

...So are <u>Disputes</u> over <u>Contracts</u>

A <u>contract</u> is an agreement between two people — they <u>both</u> promise to do something. It's often written down and signed by both parties, but you can also have a verbal agreement.

1) People have to stick to the contracts they make — <u>Contract Law</u> is part of <u>civil law</u>.

2) Loads of contracts are made in <u>everyday life</u>. E.g. if a window cleaner offers to clean your windows for a fiver, and you agree, then you and the window cleaner have made a contract.

3) When you <u>buy</u> something, you enter into a contract with the seller. If the item you bought isn't fit for purpose, your <u>Consumer Rights</u> have been infringed (see page 9), and you can take <u>civil legal action</u> (although it's sensible to try other routes first, e.g. go back to the shop and ask for a refund).

Civil Law — remember your P's and Q's...

So there you have it. Basically, <u>civil law</u>'s about solving personal disputes and tends to result in compensation being paid. <u>Criminal law</u> is more to do with general law and order, and involves punishment being meted out.

More on Civil Law

There's a bit more you need to know about <u>civil law</u>, but then we get on to the more exciting criminal stuff...

Employment Laws are Civil Laws

1) <u>Employees</u> have statutory rights — rights set out in law, e.g. the minimum wage, and the right not to be discriminated against (see page 10). They usually also have <u>contracts</u> setting out what's expected of them — if they don't do these things, they're likely to get the sack.

2) If someone believes they've been treated <u>unfairly</u>, they can take their employer to an <u>Employment Tribunal</u>.

3) <u>Trade unions</u> (see page 10) offer their members <u>legal support</u> if they have a dispute with their employer.

ASBOs are Civil Court Orders

1) <u>ASBOs</u> (Antisocial Behaviour Orders) <u>aren't</u> intended to punish wrongdoers — they're just meant to <u>stop</u> the person doing a certain thing, e.g. being noisy, begging, spitting, harassing someone.

You can be given an ASBO for something which <u>isn't</u> against the law.

2) Even though an ASBO is a <u>civil order</u>, if you break one it's a <u>crime</u> and you can go to prison for 5 years.

3) ASBOs are often associated with <u>young people</u> — but people of all ages get them, e.g. an 87-year-old man got one for shouting things rudely at his neighbours.

You Can Get Legal Support from the CAB or a Solicitor

THE CITIZENS' ADVICE BUREAU (CAB)

The Citizens' Advice Bureau is great. It provides <u>free legal advice</u> to anyone. In fact, their trained volunteers will help you solve pretty much <u>any problem</u>, from money troubles to relationship problems. Most towns have a CAB, so you can go along in person, or you can ring up for advice or even e-mail.

Deputy Sheriff Foley was happy to provide free fashion advice.

If you can't afford to pay for legal support, and you're considered to have a pretty good case, then you can get legal aid to pay the bill.

SOLICITORS

Solicitors provide <u>legal advice and help</u>, and they'll also represent you in <u>court</u> — but they usually charge a fee (and often quite a large one). Solicitors have specialist areas, e.g. family issues, employment issues, etc.

Justice Can Mean Treating People the Same or Differently

1) There are <u>differences</u> between people, so being fair sometimes means treating people <u>differently</u>.

2) The Greek philosopher Aristotle said:

> "Treat equals equally and unequals unequally."

This is still an important <u>principle of justice</u>.

3) For example, it's thought <u>fair</u> that <u>needy</u> people are given more help from the government than <u>rich</u> people, and that <u>children</u> aren't allowed to damage their health by smoking, but <u>adults</u> are.

4) Another example is that under-10s can't be convicted of a crime in England and Wales. Children younger than this aren't generally thought to know <u>right from wrong</u>. Child criminals <u>aren't</u> treated in the same way as adults either (see page 45).

In Scotland, it's under-8s (but there are plans to change it to under-12s).

5) But people should <u>only</u> be treated differently if the difference between them is <u>relevant to the situation</u>.

6) For example, if two people do the <u>same work equally well</u>, they should be paid the <u>same wage</u>. Differences in gender, race or religion <u>don't</u> matter in this case, so they shouldn't be taken into account.

No one told me the law couldn't touch me when I was 9...

In the UK, the age of criminal responsibility is a lot lower than in many other countries — in Germany and Spain it's 14, and in France you can get away with stuff 'til you're 17. Some people argue that 10 is too young — after all, you can't buy cigarettes, vote, get a tattoo and so on until you're much older.

Tackling Crime

In an <u>ideal world</u>, all criminals would be caught by the police and punished by the law, then feel really bad and never commit another crime again. Unfortunately life isn't <u>quite like that</u>. ← Well, actually, in an ideal world there'd be no crime...

People Commit Crimes for Different Reasons

There are loads of different sorts of crime — and plenty of different motives for committing them.

1) Crimes like theft, fraud, burglary and drug dealing may be done for <u>personal gain</u> of money or possessions.

2) Some crimes are carefully planned and thought about ('<u>premeditated</u>'), e.g. a large-scale bank robbery.

3) Violent crimes and criminal damage are often committed on the spur of the moment, e.g. '<u>crimes of passion</u>', caused by strong feelings like <u>jealousy</u> and <u>hatred</u>. Alternatively, the person mightn't be thinking straight at the time, e.g. they could be under the influence of <u>drugs</u> or <u>alcohol</u>, or could be <u>mentally ill</u>.

4) Some criminals even <u>get a kick</u> out of committing crimes — from people who are addicted to stealing (the posh word for this is '<u>kleptomania</u>'), to people who joy-ride cars for the <u>thrill</u>, or even <u>serial murderers</u>.

5) Being a victim of crime can cause all sorts of problems, and it can affect the victim's family too.

Whilst taking his pet crowbar for an evening stroll, Wayne noticed that the door was unlocked.

Many crimes involve a <u>loss of property or money</u>, creating <u>financial problems</u> for victims, e.g. pensioners robbed of their savings, or someone burgled who isn't insured. Some <u>sentimental</u> items can't be replaced.

With more serious crimes, like <u>murder</u>, the family and friends of the victim can find it difficult to get on with their lives again. Rape or assault can leave <u>psychological damage</u> as well as <u>physical injuries</u>.

In communities where there's a lot of crime around, it can create an atmosphere of <u>fear and mistrust</u>, which can make the problems even worse.

The Police are the Main Law Enforcers in Britain

The police have lots of <u>different roles</u>...

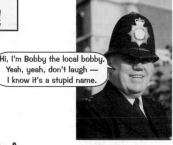

Hi, I'm Bobby the local bobby. Yeah, yeah, don't laugh — I know it's a stupid name.

1) Some communities have <u>local police officers</u> (the local 'bobbies') who patrol the area (the 'beat') on foot to make sure everything's in order. They deal with local disturbances, discourage criminals and provide a <u>reassuring presence</u>.

2) Other police officers <u>patrol in police cars</u>. The central police station takes calls from the public and sends the nearest car to the scene of the incident. They deal with problems such as car accidents, burglaries, pub brawls — whatever needs sorting out.

3) The police attend <u>big events</u>, e.g. football matches, to help them go smoothly.

4) Police detectives solve the more complicated cases. They're helped by <u>forensic scientists</u> using techniques like DNA fingerprinting, which allows scientists to match samples of blood, hair and so on taken from the scene of the crime with samples taken from suspects.

There are other special types of police — e.g. <u>armed police</u>, who carry guns, and <u>crowd control police</u>, who wear armour and sometimes ride horses.

5) If the police <u>suspect</u> that someone has committed a crime, they have the power to <u>arrest</u> them and haul them off to the police station for <u>questioning</u>. There's more on this on the next page.

6) The police also advise people on how to <u>prevent</u> crime, and support <u>educational programmes</u>, e.g. by visiting schools to talk about issues such as personal safety and drugs.

When I were a lad we didn' even 'ave a front door te lock...

Eeeee... it's nasty stuff all this criminal activity. And once the police have figured out whodunnit, and arrested the criminal, it's far from the end of the matter. They have to give evidence in court to show how they're so sure they've got the right person. There's lots about the court system coming up on page 43...

The Criminal Justice System

The police <u>don't</u> have unlimited power, and they certainly can't lock 'em up and throw away the key.
There are <u>strict rules</u> about how they operate — and it's not even actually them who prosecutes offenders.

There's a Procedure to be Followed when a Suspect is Caught

Here's what'd happen if you were arrested for a crime:

The Police Will Arrest, Question and Charge You

1) If the police have reason to think you've committed a crime, they'll <u>arrest</u> you.

2) You'll be taken to the police station and <u>questioned</u> for up to <u>24 hours</u>. You <u>don't</u> have to answer their questions (but this might look dodgy and count against you in court — you'll be treated more sympathetically if you're <u>honest</u>).
   Lying to them's a <u>really</u> bad idea (you'll be committing the offence of <u>obstructing a police officer</u>).

If the police have good reason to believe you've done something really bad, then they can apply to a magistrate to get this extended.

3) You have the right to see a <u>solicitor</u> free of charge. And if you're <u>under 17</u>, the police can't question you unless a parent, guardian, or other adult who knows you (e.g. a teacher) is there.

But if it's a minor offence and you've never done anything like it before, you <u>might</u> be lucky and get off with a caution.

4) If the police reckon they have enough evidence, they'll <u>charge</u> you (formally accuse you of the crime).

Then You'll be Remanded on Bail or in Custody

1) Next you'll appear at a <u>magistrates' court</u> (or a youth court), where your charge is read out.

2) You'll usually be <u>remanded on bail</u> — this means you'll be <u>released</u> until your trial. To make sure you don't do a runner, they often ask for some <u>money</u> to be put up as a guarantee. If you show up in court, the money is given back; if you don't they keep it.

3) If the magistrate thinks there's a good chance you'll reoffend or won't show up (usually if it's a really serious crime), you'll be <u>remanded in custody</u> until your trial (this means you'll be put in prison).

The CPS Decides Whether to Prosecute

1) It's the <u>Crown Prosecution Service</u> (CPS) who decide whether someone should be prosecuted. The Crown Prosecution Service was set up <u>separately</u> from the police to try to make the system <u>fair</u>.

2) The Crown Prosecution Service look at the <u>evidence</u> and decide if it's strong enough to prove you did the crime. They'll only prosecute if they think there's a <u>better than 50-50 chance</u> of <u>conviction</u>, and if the crime is <u>serious enough</u> for taking it to court to be in the <u>public interest</u> (court cases cost heaps of money).

If the Crown Prosecution Service <u>do</u> decide to prosecute, then your next stop is <u>court</u>. See the next page.

The Criminals Get Away with It All Too Often

1) A crime is defined as '<u>detected</u>' if a suspect is <u>charged</u> for it.

2) Only a shocking <u>27%</u> of <u>reported crimes</u> in England and Wales were detected in 2005-6.

The detection rate varies a lot between offences. 95% of reported drug offences were detected, but only 14% of burglaries.

3) Some people reckon that the detection rate is <u>so low</u> because the police have to do so much <u>paperwork</u>, so don't have time to get out and catch criminals.

4) To make things worse, <u>less than half</u> of crimes are even reported, making the true detection rate <u>far lower</u>. There are lots of reasons why people don't report crimes, e.g.:

- They don't believe the police will be able to <u>catch</u> the person.
- They're <u>embarrassed</u> (maybe if there's been a sexual offence committed).
- If it's someone they know who committed the offence, they may want to <u>protect</u> them.

What puddings do policemen like? — Custardy ones...

When someone's arrested, their right to freedom is infringed. It might be that they are totally innocent, but on balance, it's considered better for society as a whole if the police can hold suspects and question them.

The Criminal Justice System

The <u>Universal Declaration of Human Rights</u> (see p.3) says that everyone should have the right to a <u>fair trial</u> — and this happens in court where evidence is examined, and suspects get the chance to defend themselves.

Courts Decide if a Suspect is Guilty or Innocent

There are two main types of court — magistrates' courts and crown courts.

Nearly All Criminal Cases are Dealt with in Magistrates' Court

1) Someone who is going to be prosecuted goes to a <u>magistrates' court</u>. They're called the <u>defendant</u>, and normally have a <u>lawyer</u>.

> Unless they're under 18 — then they go to a youth court. See page 45.

2) <u>Magistrates</u> are also known as Lay Justices, Justices of the Peace or JPs. They're respected members of the community who are <u>part-time</u> and <u>unpaid</u>. There'll be two or three magistrates on each case and they're advised on the law by a legally-qualified court clerk.

3) <u>District judges</u> are similar to magistrates but they're <u>experienced lawyers</u> and work <u>alone</u>, usually on more complicated cases.

> There's no jury in a magistrates' court.

4) The defendant will be asked to give a plea of <u>guilty</u> or <u>not guilty</u>.

If they plead GUILTY...

The defendant's lawyer usually tries to persuade the magistrates to give a <u>light sentence</u> — perhaps by explaining the reason why they committed the crime.

The magistrates decide what the punishment will be — this is called <u>sentencing</u>.

If they plead NOT GUILTY...

There'll be a <u>trial</u>. Crown Prosecution Service lawyers will <u>question witnesses</u> and make statements to try to persuade the magistrate that the defendant is guilty. The defendant's lawyer will do the same — but to try to show the defendant is innocent.

The magistrates then decide if the defendant <u>is</u> guilty, and pass a <u>sentence</u> if they are.

5) A magistrates' court can give a fine of <u>up to £5000</u>, or prison sentences of up to <u>6 months per offence</u>.

More Serious Cases are Dealt with in the Crown Court (this is the type where the judges wear wigs)

1) If the case is <u>very serious</u> (e.g. murder, rape, arson), the magistrate will refer it on to the <u>crown court</u>.

2) A trial in a crown court is similar to a trial in a magistrates' court, with witnesses being questioned, and statements being made. But in a crown court, a <u>jury</u> decides whether the defendant is guilty.

- A <u>jury</u> is made up of 12 adults aged 18-70.
- They represent a <u>cross-section</u> of the general public, to make sure that fair decisions are made.
- <u>Anyone</u> (except people with criminal records or mental illnesses) can be summoned for jury service.
- Jurors <u>have to</u> attend for as long as is required, unless there's a very good reason. It can be an interesting experience. Some payments are made, to cover expenses and loss of earnings.

3) At least <u>ten</u> jury members have to agree with the decision. The judge <u>advises the jury</u> and decides on the <u>punishment</u> if the defendant is found guilty.

Fact of the day — a judge's mallet is called a gavel...

The wheels of justice mustn't be stopped from turning — lying in court is called <u>perjury</u> and can get you seven years in prison. Doing something that might prevent a fair trial is known as <u>contempt of court</u>. This could be anything from swearing at the judge, to publishing material that might sway the jury.

Punishment

There's a range of punishments that courts can dish out to offenders...

There are Different Types of Punishment for Lawbreakers

FINES For reasonably underlined minor crimes, such as speeding, the offender might get away with a underlined fine.

COMMUNITY SENTENCES These are made up of different elements, chosen to suit the offender.

E.g.:
- underlined unpaid work — e.g. clearing up litter.
- underlined curfew — e.g. they have to be inside their house by 9 pm. They might have an electronic tag around their ankle to check they obey their curfew.
- underlined bans from certain places — e.g. a football hooligan could be banned from matches.
- underlined having to attend special programmes — e.g. to get them off drugs or alcohol.

RESTORATIVE JUSTICE This involves the underlined offender and victim communicating with each other, with the help of a trained mediator. It gives the victim a chance to explain how the crime has underlined affected them, and the offender a chance to underlined apologise and underlined explain their actions.

> The average 'lifer' actually serves about 14 years, but some are never released.

PRISON Major crimes mean a trip to underlined prison. Sentences vary from a few weeks to life (they can be reduced if criminals show underlined remorse and are well-behaved in prison).

There are Four Main Purposes of Prison Sentences

Prison's aren't *just* a way of getting criminals off the streets. Here are the main reasons why they're used:

1) underlined DETERRENCE — the threat of being sent to prison should underlined put people off committing crime in the first place. And hopefully, if people have served one prison sentence, they should be deterred from getting into trouble again and ending up back 'inside'. But, as you'll see below, it doesn't seem to work that way.

2) underlined PROTECTION — The public need to be protected from underlined dangerous criminals.

3) underlined REFORM AND REHABILITATION — prisons are meant to help people become underlined useful members of society. Prisoners may be given underlined education and training so they're more likely to get a underlined job when they get out.

4) underlined RETRIBUTION — Some people think prison sentences are a way of making offenders 'underlined pay' for what they did. The idea is, their crimes harmed others, so they should have an equal amount of harm done to them.

Over Half of Ex-Prisoners Reoffend

The underlined RECIDIVISM RATE is the percentage of people who are punished for crimes and then reoffend.

1) For people who've been in your average prison, the recidivism rate is underlined more than 50%. There are underlined lots of reasons why ex-prisoners reoffend:

- While in prison, they meet other criminals (often much more serious ones) — this is a underlined bad influence on them.
- Being in prison underlined disrupts their lives — they're likely to lose their job, and possibly even their home and family. This makes them underlined more likely to reoffend.
- Crime is often linked to underlined social background — crime levels are always higher in underlined deprived areas (often inner cities) where there's poverty, gangs and drug problems. If people go back to these areas, they're likely to get involved in crime again.

> Prevention is better than cure — many people believe that addressing social problems, e.g. through urban regeneration projects, is the best way to reduce crime.

2) People who are punished by community sentences are less likely to reoffend. This is possibly because community sentences underlined disrupt their lives underlined less.

Prison — the naughty step for grown-ups...

Some people think that the government is soft on crime, and that's why there's so much of it. But money is an issue — it costs a huge amount to keep someone in prison, and there are only a limited number of cells.

YOTs and Probation Services

The UK justice system spends a lot of time and money trying to <u>help</u> offenders so that they don't <u>reoffend</u>. <u>Youth Offending Teams (YOTs)</u> and <u>probation services</u> play really important roles in this.

The <u>Youth Justice System</u> Deals with <u>Youth Crime</u>

1) <u>Youth crime</u> is common in Britain — factors such as a troubled home life, doing badly in school, living in poverty, drug or alcohol use, and peer group pressure make a young person more likely to commit a crime.

2) Criminals who are <u>under 18 years old</u> are dealt with in youth courts — a <u>division</u> of the magistrates' court.

3) Youth courts have <u>specially trained magistrates</u> and are <u>less formal</u> than adult courts. Members of the public aren't allowed in to watch.

4) For really serious offences such as murder, a young person might have to go to the <u>crown court</u> instead of the youth court.

They were sent to the youth court for serious fashion crimes.

Prison is a <u>Last Resort</u> for Young Offenders

1) If it's your first offence and you plead guilty, you'll often get a <u>referral order</u>. This means you'll have to meet with a panel to agree how you could put right any harm you've done.

2) Alternatively, you might get a <u>community sentence</u> (see page 44). This is most likely if you're 16 or 17.

3) Offenders may also be given <u>ASBOs</u> (Antisocial Behaviour Orders) — see page 40.

4) Persistent or fairly serious young offenders get <u>Detention and Training Orders</u> (DTOs) of up to 2 years. Some of this time is spent in <u>custody</u>, and some under <u>supervision in the community</u>.

5) They may be put in <u>Young Offenders' Institutions</u> or <u>Secure Children's Homes</u>, but never adult prisons. Wherever young offenders end up, they don't just sit behind bars. There's lots of emphasis on <u>education</u>, <u>vocational training</u> and courses aimed to <u>improve</u> their behaviour.

<u>Youth Offending Teams</u> are Part of the <u>Youth Justice System</u>

1) <u>Youth Offending Teams (YOTs)</u> are made up of people from a wide variety of organisations — the police, social services, the probation service, health services, etc. They're organised by <u>local authorities</u>.

2) YOTs play a key role in <u>all parts</u> of the youth justice system. For example:

- The police call the YOT after arresting a young person so that the offender can receive <u>support</u>.
- The YOT provide the court with <u>information</u> about the young person that may affect the case.
- YOTs <u>supervise</u> young offenders who are carrying out their <u>sentences</u>, e.g <u>community service</u>.
- YOTs <u>assess</u> each young offender and develop a programme to help them avoid <u>reoffending</u>.

The <u>Probation Service</u> Supervises Community Sentences

1) If an offender's given a community sentence, the <u>National Probation Service</u> make sure they do it.

2) It also works with prisoners and ex-prisoners to help them <u>reintegrate</u> back into society.

3) Before an offender is released, the Probation Service will provide a <u>report</u> to the prison bosses about any risks they pose to society, and whether they should have a <u>curfew</u>, be <u>electronically tagged</u>, or have to report to a <u>Probation Officer</u> every week.

4) Problems like <u>unemployment</u> and <u>homelessness</u> make offenders more likely to end up back in prison. The Probation Service try to tackle these issues by <u>running hostels</u>, and <u>arranging courses</u> in basic English and maths.

More than two-thirds of prisoners can't do maths as well as the average 11-year-old.

Youth offending is easy — make 'em stay in and revise...

...oh no, that's offending youths... Anyway, whether you're offended by it or not, you do need to know it.

Quick Test

'Ello, 'ello, 'ello, what 'ave we 'ere then...

A load more questions for you to answer, that's what. It's the best way of testing what you can remember and making sure you know your judges from your juries. So have a bash at these questions, check your answers and then have another go at any of the ones you weren't so sure about.
Keep doing this till you're confident you know it all.

1) Give a definition of law.

2) Why is it against the law to smoke in a public place?

3) Give an example of how a law protects people's human rights.

4) Other than protecting people's rights, give two other purposes of laws.

5) What is a Bill in Parliament?

6) What happens at the Committee Stage?

7) Do Bills usually go through the House of Commons or the House of Lords first?

8) What has to happen before the Bill becomes an Act of Parliament?

9) What is meant by the term 'common law'?

10) Give two examples of how conflicts of rights can be resolved by the law.

11) Give two ways in which civil law differs from criminal law.

12) Which type of law deals with adoptions?

13) What does ASBO stand for? Explain what one is.

14) Name two sources of legal support and advice.

15) What does justice mean? a) treating everyone equally
                              b) treating everyone differently
                              c) treating everyone fairly

16) What is a 'premeditated crime'?

17) Apart from arresting bad 'uns, give three different roles of the police.

18) How long can the police hold someone they've arrested for questioning?

19) What does it mean if someone is 'remanded on bail'?

20) What does it mean if someone is 'remanded in custody'?

21) Whose job is it to prosecute offenders?

22) Give an example of why not all crimes are reported to the police.

23) What crimes are dealt with by magistrates' courts?

24) What is a jury?

25) Who can be called for jury service?

26) What type of court has a jury?

27) What type of court has a net in the middle?

28) List three things that could be included in a community sentence.

29) What is 'restorative justice'?

30) What are the four main purposes of prison sentences?

31) What is the 'recidivism rate'?

32) Give one reason why ex-prisoners are likely to reoffend.

33) Name two types of punishments that may be given to a young offender.

34) What is the role of Youth Offending Teams (YOTs)?

35) Whose job is it to supervise community sentences and reintegrate offenders back into society?

Forms of Government

Governments come in all shapes and sizes — and some are fairer than others.

Governments **can be** Democratic **or** Non-Democratic

Democratic governments (e.g. UK, USA, France, Germany)

1) There's a choice of political parties, e.g. the Republicans and the Democrats in the USA.
2) Elections are held regularly. Representatives are elected by the people to be a voice for them.
3) Official groups are set up to monitor the work of democratic governments.

> Democracies can be...
> * A Republic — a country with no monarch. The head of the country is an elected president, e.g. USA.
> * A Constitutional Monarchy — a country that has a king or queen with limited powers, but is mostly run by an elected government, e.g. UK.

Non-democratic governments (e.g. Vietnam, People's Republic of China, Cuba)

1) There's often only one political party. The government's powers are not limited.
2) The public don't get to elect the government.
3) Media is often controlled, ensuring only pro-government information is communicated.
4) Any opposition is suppressed. Opposition leaders are often imprisoned or worse.
5) Power can be imposed using the military.

> Non-democratic governments can be...
> * Absolute Monarchies — rule by a king or queen, who inherited the position. More common in the past.
> * Dictatorships — rule by a single unelected leader who may use force to keep control, e.g. North Korea.
> * Totalitarian Rule — a country with a single ruling political party, such as China.

E.g. in 1989 the Chinese authorities used the army to stop protests in Tiananmen Square, Beijing. This resulted in hundreds of deaths.

Democratic Parliaments **Keep a Check** on Governments

In a democracy, it's the job of Parliament to ensure government is fair and just — this is called Scrutiny.

1) Debates provide an open forum for views to be shared. The opposition parties question the actions of the government.

   In the UK you can see this during Prime Minister's Questions — it's broadcast on TV (and radio).

2) Select committees are set up to investigate and report on departments or particular issues. They're made up of MPs from all the parties.

   E.g. in 2009 in the UK the Standards Committee investigated the scandal surrounding MPs' expense claims, which led to some ministers resigning their posts and some MPs not standing for re-election.

3) If a government is seen as ineffective, a 'vote of no confidence' can be called for — if Parliament votes against the government, the government usually has to call a general election or resign.

Human Rights **Often Suffer in** Non-Democratic **Systems**

1) In a single-party system with no opposition there's little debate, and few checks on the government.

> The government may listen to different opinions, but can ignore them. E.g. the National People's Congress (China's parliament) only passes legislation that the ruling Communist Party has approved. Corruption often goes unchallenged — it leads to distrust and systems that are unfair.

One choice of party: limiting

2) In a dictatorship, fear often replaces trust, as dictators can do anything they want.

> Because opposition is suppressed, no debate occurs and decisions go unchallenged. Laws are often passed without any approval from a parliament. Many decisions are kept secret.

Dictators: bossy

E.g. the North Korean dictator has ordered that all triplets be taken from their parents and put in orphanages. He said it was to help the poor, but everyone believes it's because Korean superstition says that triplets may rise to positions of power, and he's worried he'll be toppled.

I once called for a 'vote of no confidence' in my mum's spinach lasagne...

At the start of the 20th century, Europe was dominated by monarchies like Russia and Austria-Hungary. After two World Wars and a Cold War it's all a democracy — it seems people don't like being bossed around.

Levels of Government

The UK is a <u>representative democracy</u> — we choose <u>representatives</u> (MPs) to <u>run the country</u> on our behalf. And we also get to choose who we want to run our <u>local</u> area on our behalf, too.

Local Governments **Make** Local Decisions

1) The national government is the <u>central government</u>. It makes all the decisions that affect the <u>whole country</u>, e.g. about <u>health</u>, <u>defence</u> and <u>environmental</u> affairs.

2) Some powers are passed to <u>local governments</u>, e.g. <u>education</u>, <u>housing</u>, <u>transport</u> and <u>social services</u>. This is because local governments are better placed to make <u>appropriate decisions</u> for the <u>local area</u> to meet <u>local people's needs</u>.

3) Local governments are run by <u>councillors</u>, who are <u>elected</u> every four years. Most councillors represent <u>political parties</u>, but some are <u>independent</u>.

Local governments are also called councils or authorities.

4) Councillors choose a <u>Leader of the Council</u>, who is in charge of political matters.

5) A <u>Mayor</u> (Lord Mayor in big cities) is chosen each year to be the <u>ceremonial head</u> of the council. Mayors have limited power but are the <u>public face of the council</u> and do official, ceremonial stuff, like open new buildings.

Mwah, pomp, mwah, ra-ra, ceremony, tally-ho, yah, what?

6) Local councils <u>raise</u> half their money through <u>council tax</u> (see page 21), and <u>central government</u> provide the other half.

The <u>biggest chunk</u> of money — about a <u>third</u> of the total — is spent on <u>education</u>.

Local Government **can be** Single-Tier **or** Two-Tier

1) <u>Smaller towns</u> and <u>rural areas</u> in England use a <u>two-tier system</u>: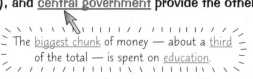

This is to try to make councils more <u>efficient</u> and <u>in touch</u> with local people.

- <u>County councils</u> are responsible for big things like <u>education</u> and <u>strategic planning</u>.
- Each county is divided into districts — <u>district councils</u> look after things like <u>waste collection</u> and <u>housing</u>.

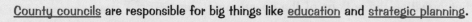

2) Some areas of England also have small <u>parish</u> or <u>town councils</u>, with limited responsibilities. They look after <u>local issues</u> like <u>street lighting</u>.

3) Other parts of England (usually the <u>big cities</u>) have a <u>single-tier system</u> of local government (also called a <u>unitary system</u>) where the <u>Unitary</u> or <u>Metropolitan Authority</u> looks after all the local services.

4) Wales and Scotland use the single-tier system too.

London **has Its Own** Local Government

1) London's local government system is a <u>bit different</u> because London is so big. It's made up of '<u>the City</u>' (a self-governing business district), <u>32 boroughs</u> and the <u>Greater London Authority</u> (GLA).

2) The GLA is the <u>city-wide</u> government which coordinates the 32 boroughs and 'the City'. It's made up of the <u>Mayor of London</u>, who is elected every four years, and <u>25 members</u> of the <u>London Assembly</u>, who <u>scrutinise</u> the decisions made by the Mayor.

3) The Mayor of London has a range of <u>specific powers</u>. He sets the <u>budget</u> for the <u>GLA</u> and the <u>Metropolitan Police</u>, and sets out <u>plans and policies for London</u> (covering things like transport, housing, economic development, culture, health inequalities and some environmental issues).

What do councillors have for lunch — tuna mayor-naise sarnies...

You deserve a medal for learning about all this <u>local government</u> lark. Or maybe even a big mayor chain. Try to find out what sort of local council covers <u>your area</u> and what they're <u>responsible</u> for. If you really want to.

What is Parliament?

How the UK is governed has changed over the years. The sovereign (king or queen) used to have loads more power. But now most of the power is in Parliament — the Queen is more of a figurehead.

There are Three Parts to Parliament

Parliament is the body which makes and changes laws in the UK. It has three parts...

House of Commons

The House of Commons is made up of elected MPs (Members of Parliament) who debate and vote on policies.
They're the folk who sit in the posh building and shout "hear hear" and stuff.

The Queen

The Queen is the official head of Parliament, but doesn't have any real power any more.

House of Lords

The House of Lords is now mostly made up of members chosen by the government (people used to inherit the right to sit there). They examine and recommend changes to Bills from the House of Commons.
They're the folk who sit in the posh building, rant, shout "hear hear" and are sometimes caught napping on TV.

Parliament Questions and Regulates the Government

The main roles of Parliament are to:

① Debate Government Policies

1) Debates in Parliament help MPs and Lords to reach an informed decision on something, like a new policy or a change in the law.

2) It gives MPs and Lords the opportunity to challenge decisions and voice any concerns — either their own or ones that have been brought to their attention by members of their constituency (see p. 50).

3) Debates are like big arguments really, only with less bad language. And there are rules to follow too:

- A debate is chaired by a Speaker. Their role is to keep order, remain impartial (not show favouritism to one political party) and to call MPs to speak.
- The Speaker calls MPs from different parties to argue their point in the debate in turn. The MPs address their speeches to the Speaker.
- At the end of the debate, MPs take a vote to resolve the debate (e.g. should taxes be increased).

Lords also take part in debates, but it's a bit less formal — the Lord Speaker chairs the debates, but the Lords manage the debates themselves and directly address each other.

② Scrutinise the Government

1) It's the job of Parliament to scrutinise the government so that the party in power can't start dictating policies or abusing its power — see page 47.

2) The Opposition Parties (see next page) keep the government in check and make sure any bad decisions are brought to the public's attention. This is important for a fair, transparent system of government.

Always wear protective clothing when investigating government policy.

Check your spelling of GoverNment and ParliAment...*

Just because the government runs the country, that doesn't mean it's perfect and never does anything wrong. Parliament is like the annoying babysitter that checks up on it to make sure it's not up to any mischief.

*Not a funny joke, admittedly, but I thought it was worth pointing out.
You wouldn't want to spell them wrong in a letter to your MP/an exam now, would you.

The Government

MPs don't just sit around all day arguing. Not every day, anyway.

The Government Manages the Country

1) The government's role is to manage the country by making new laws, setting taxes, spending money on public services, etc.

2) The leader of the party with the most MPs becomes Prime Minister — the Head of the Government.

3) The Prime Minister chooses a Minister to run each of the main government departments, e.g. defence, education, foreign policy.

4) The top 20 or so Ministers form the Cabinet. They include the minister responsible for the economy (called the Chancellor of the Exchequer) and those that run other important departments (Secretaries of State, e.g. the Secretary of State for Health).

5) The Cabinet meets each week to discuss events and plan things, e.g. what to spend money on, which ideas to try and make into laws, whether to make changes in how organisations the government's in charge of (e.g. the NHS, the police) are run.

6) Cabinet Ministers are expected not to undermine the Prime Minister by publicly disagreeing. If they disagree strongly, they sometimes end up resigning.

E.g. Robin Cook was a Labour Cabinet Minister who resigned in 2003 over the decision to go to war with Iraq.

The Prime Minister finally got a Cabinet that would do exactly what she wanted.

7) The Prime Minister sometimes changes who's in charge of the various departments (called a "cabinet reshuffle").

Opposition Parties Debate with the Government

1) The Opposition is the main political party who aren't in government. (If Labour are in government then it's usually the Conservatives, and vice versa — see the next page.)

2) Their role is to debate with the government, scrutinise government decisions and highlight weaknesses. They present alternatives — usually their own policies of what they'd do if they won the next general election.

3) The Leader of the Opposition picks a Shadow Cabinet who closely follow the work of the government's Cabinet (see above).

E.g. you often hear the Shadow Chancellor of the Exchequer arguing against tax increases and public spending plans, and saying what they'd do if only you'd give them the chance...

4) Some people think that having opposition parties can lead to arguing for argument's sake. This can put people off politics and waste a government's time.

All MPs Represent Their Constituents in Parliament

Hello? I'd like to reduce tax on hair gel.

1) MPs represent all their constituents in Parliament — whether they voted for them or not.

2) You can write to, email or phone your MP with problems that the government's responsible for, from rules on school admissions to nuclear defence policy (but not council services). MPs also hold surgeries in their constituencies where you can meet them face to face.

3) Your MP can contact the minister responsible, or raise the matter in a debate in Parliament. This publicises the issue, and forces the minister responsible to consider it and defend their actions.

E.g. on Prime Minister's questions (see page 47), you might hear MPs ask the Prime Minister for help if a factory is threatened with closure (maybe by providing government loans to help keep the factory open, or money to help retrain workers that get made redundant).

4) You can use the internet to find out who your local MP is and what they have been doing.

Musical chairs at political parties...

Yeah, yeah, politics — boring, yawn. But politics affects you more than you might think. You need to know the facts about the government, the Cabinet and what MPs can do for you — this page gives you the basics.

Voting

There are a couple of important ways that people can participate in democracy. One is to be a <u>member</u> of a political party. The easier way is to <u>vote</u> — and help decide which political party runs the government.

Most MPs <u>Belong to</u> Political Parties

There are also a few <u>Independent MPs</u> who don't belong to a party.

1) Political parties are organisations of <u>like-minded</u> people who try to get representatives elected to <u>Parliament</u>. There are three main parties in Britain (and a few small parties too, such as the <u>Green Party</u>):

<u>Labour</u> are associated with policies aimed at <u>social welfare</u> and equality.

<u>Conservative</u> policies are usually aimed at helping businesses and <u>lowering taxes</u>.

The <u>Liberal Democrats</u> have many <u>pro-freedom</u> and <u>pro-environment</u> policies.

2) The party with the <u>most MPs elected</u> is the government. If it's <u>Labour</u>, the <u>Conservatives</u> are the <u>official opposition</u>, and vice versa (because the <u>Liberal Democrats</u> are usually the <u>third most popular</u> party).

3) General elections result in <u>fierce competition</u> between parties:

- Before an election, each party publishes their <u>manifesto</u> — a document outlining their policies, i.e. <u>what they'll do if they're elected</u>. Other parties will criticise their proposals, and say what they'd do <u>instead</u>.
- Party members <u>canvass</u> (ask for votes) <u>locally</u> through door-to-door meetings with members of the public, posters, flyers and adverts. Canvassing's also done <u>nationally</u> through articles, reports and advertising that promote the party's manifesto on <u>TV</u>, <u>radio</u> and in the <u>newspapers</u>.

4) <u>Anyone</u> can become a member of a political party — pay the <u>annual fee</u> and you're in. Party members can be involved in <u>choosing</u> their <u>local candidates</u>, and can help decide on <u>policies</u>.

Most UK Elections use a First-Past-the-Post System

1) The whole of the UK is divided up into <u>646</u> voting areas known as <u>constituencies</u>. Each constituency has around <u>70 000 voters</u>.

2) The 'first-past-the-post' system means that the candidate with the <u>most votes</u> in a constituency becomes the <u>MP</u> to represent everyone in the constituency.

3) The party with the most 'seats' out of the 646 becomes the <u>government</u>.

Two-Party System = Two-Horse Race

The <u>first-past-the-post system</u> means that elections are usually a race between the <u>two main parties</u> — <u>Labour</u> and the <u>Conservatives</u>. This has good and bad points...

Compare this with proportional representation on p. 53.

ADVANTAGES
- With only two main parties there's usually a <u>clear winner</u>. A government with a large majority finds it <u>easier</u> to get new laws passed (and actually get stuff done).
- There's a strong <u>Opposition</u> whose job is to <u>challenge</u> the government and debate issues <u>before laws are made</u>.

DISADVANTAGES
- Sometimes the party with the <u>most votes</u> might <u>not</u> win the <u>most seats</u>, so it doesn't get into power.
- <u>Smaller parties</u> might get lots of votes spread across all the constituencies but if they don't get the majority in many constituencies, they won't win many seats. So they don't get much <u>say in Parliament</u>.
- <u>Minority views</u> may not be well-represented by the two main parties.
- If you vote in a constituency that tends to have a <u>big majority</u> of voters for <u>one party</u> (a "<u>safe seat</u>") your vote is <u>less likely</u> to affect the <u>overall outcome</u> than a vote in a <u>marginal constituency</u> (where it's a <u>tight contest</u>). Even safe seats do change hands sometimes though.

At breakfast I use a First-Pass-the-Toast system...
Parties, horse racing — see, it's already more interesting than you thought it would be. So get learning...

More on Voting

No, not Moron Voting... You need to know about how people get to vote and about mock elections.
There's something else important, what was it... oh, I dunno, I don't really care. Something about apathy.

You Need to be on the Electoral Register to Vote

1) Local councils (see p. 48) compile the electoral register (or roll) every year around October.

2) Before the election each voter is sent a polling card. They have to choose one of the people listed on the card (usually a member of a political party) to represent them.

3) Voting happens at polling stations — somewhere local with easy access, such as a village hall, though you can also vote by post.

4) Voting is secret so it's fair — you can't be bullied into voting for one particular candidate.

> **ELECTIONS IN THE UK**
> * European Elections
> * General Elections (government)
> * Regional Elections (regional government)
> * Local Elections (councils)
> * Referendums (votes on single issues)
> * By-elections (held between general elections to elect a new MP to a constituency, e.g. if the previous MP resigns).

Voter Apathy is when People Can't be Bothered

1) Almost 40% of the people allowed to vote in a general election don't vote. In European elections turnout is usually even lower.

2) Voting gives you a say in how the country is run, but lots of (especially young) people aren't interested in politics. Some think that none of the parties represent their views, others reckon that their vote won't change anything.

3) Some people think that it should be mandatory (required by law) for everyone to vote. But others think that this is against true democracy because it takes away freedom of choice.

4) Low turnout can be a problem — it can allow minority parties with extreme views to gain power (they're often better at getting their supporters to vote).

5) Some people think that the voting age should be lowered to 16, because it's unfair that 16-year-olds are allowed to marry and have children, work and pay taxes, and join the armed forces, but not vote.

6) Others (including over half of 16-18 year olds) disagree. They say that 16-year-olds are easily influenced, or not mature or experienced enough to take everything that political parties say into account.

Mock Elections Recreate Elections in Schools

"I say, you there — vote Silly Uniform Party!"

1) Mock elections are a way for pupils to vote as if they were taking part in general elections.

2) There's a website where schools can submit their results at the same time as the real election, to see who under-18s across the country would have elected.

3) They encourage students to take an interest in politics and to learn how the system works. You can even stand as a candidate and run a campaign if you want.

4) You might also have had the chance to vote on things within your school — e.g. which charity to support, or who should be class representative for a school council.

Mock Elections — Not just poking fun at voters...

In general elections, your vote is your way to have a say in how the country is run — and it's a right that people have died fighting for. Voting in an election shows that you think this right is important.

Changes to Democracy

Devolution is just a posh word for handing over power — in this case, to the different countries of the UK.

Political Power Has Been Decentralised and Devolved

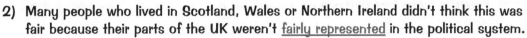

1) Government in the UK used to be very centralised — we were ruled only from London.

2) Many people who lived in Scotland, Wales or Northern Ireland didn't think this was fair because their parts of the UK weren't fairly represented in the political system.

3) A referendum (see below) was held to see how many people wanted more political control over decisions affecting their own country. This happened in 1997 in Scotland and Wales, and 1998 in Northern Ireland.

4) Scotland and Wales voted for separate regional governments, so some powers were devolved (handed over) from London government to regional assemblies.

5) Political disagreements meant the Northern Ireland Assembly was suspended in 2002, but the main parties agreed to continue power-sharing in 2007.

Regional Assemblies Don't Have Complete Control

Not all powers have been devolved to regional assemblies — things like taxation are still decided in London, and the regions still elect Westminster MPs in general elections. Each assembly has different things they control:

Scottish Parliament

- Based in Edinburgh
- Controls most policy within Scotland, except monetary policy and foreign affairs
- Sets taxes (income taxes must stay within 3% of England's)
- Makes its own laws

National Assembly for Wales

- Based in Cardiff
- Has its own budget
- Controls education, health, agriculture, housing, economic development and transport
- Makes its own laws (since 2007)
- Has limited tax-setting powers (e.g. prescription costs and elderly care)

Northern Ireland Assembly

- Based in Stormont — Belfast
- Controls health, education and local government and makes laws about these.
- Works with Republic of Ireland on same-interest matters such as transport and agriculture

Assemblies Use Proportional Representation

1) Proportional representation (PR) is used instead of 'first-past-the-post' (see p. 51) to elect assembly representatives. Many people think that PR is fairer, because every vote counts. PR helps to make sure that the number of seats for each party actually reflects the number of people who voted for them.

2) Some people don't like PR because it means voting for a party rather than a specific person. It often leads to coalitions — government shared between two or more parties, which sometimes don't work together.

3) In the Northern Ireland Assembly, each party gets a share of the seats in proportion to the number of votes. In the Scottish Parliament and National Assembly for Wales, citizens get one vote for a candidate and one for a party.

Referendums are When People are Asked to Vote on an Issue

1) A referendum is when an important issue is decided by getting people to vote directly for or against it.

- It's often about changing the way the country is governed, e.g. should there be a new regional or national assembly.
- It's also used to make sure people agree to a big, expensive plan, e.g. in 2008 Greater Manchester residents were asked if they wanted to pay for improved public transport by bringing in a congestion charge for driving at rush hour. They didn't.

2) Some people think that referendums shouldn't be used too much — because governments wouldn't get very much done, and people would get tired of voting for things they'd elected a government to decide.

Devolution — it doesn't mean MPs turning into chimps...

Believe it or not, there was a referendum in North-East England in 2004 — on whether the North-East should have a regional assembly. But 78% of people said no thanks, they didn't want any more politicians.

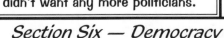

Quick Test

Seeing as you've gone to the trouble of reading this section, you may as well see if you remember any of it. Even if you have zero interest in politics, it'll mean that if you're at a really boring dinner party in the future, at least you'll know what everyone is going on about (and it might come up in the exam).

The best way to make sure you're a big know-it-all is to have a go at answering these lovely questions.

1) Give two differences between democratic and non-democratic governments.
2) What is the difference between a republic and a constitutional monarchy?
3) What is the difference between a dictatorship and totalitarian rule?
4) What is government scrutiny?
5) What is a select committee?
6) What is a 'vote of no confidence'?
7) Why are human rights more likely to suffer in non-democratic systems of government?
8) What kind of powers do local governments have?
9) Name two ways in which local councils get their money.
10) What is the difference between the single-tier and the two-tier systems of local government?
11) Describe London's system of local government.
12) What kind of powers does the Mayor of London have?
13) Which two houses make up Parliament?
14) How does Parliament represent the general public?
15) What is the purpose of debates in Parliament?
16) What is the role of the government?
17) What is the Cabinet and what do they do?
18) What is the role of the Opposition Party?
19) What does MP stand for? What do MPs do?
20) What are the three main political parties in Britain?
21) Who can be a member of a political party?
22) What's a 'constituency'? How many are there?
23) Explain how the 'first-past-the-post' system works.
24) Give two advantages and two disadvantages of having a two-party system.
25) Name three types of elections held in the UK.
26) What is meant by the term 'voter apathy'?
27) Why do some people think that 16 and 17 year olds should have a vote? Why do others disagree?
28) What does devolution of power mean?
29) Name the regional governments in Scotland, Wales and Northern Ireland. Name a power each has.
30) Why is proportional representation seen as a fairer system than 'first-past-the-post' by some people?
31) What is a referendum?

The Media and Democracy

Believe it or not, the media isn't just there so you can catch up on the latest celebrity gossip. It's a really important part of a <u>democracy</u> as it <u>communicates information</u>, letting us know what's going on in the world.

There are Different Types of Media

There are three main types of media:

1) <u>Print</u> — printed media is also known as <u>press</u>. It includes <u>magazines</u>, <u>newspapers</u> and <u>books</u>.
2) <u>Broadcast</u> — broadcast media is, erm, anything that's broadcast. It includes <u>TV</u>, <u>radio</u> and <u>cinema</u>.
3) <u>ICT</u> — The most common form of ICT media is the <u>internet</u>, but there are also CD-ROMs, podcasts, etc.

The media operates on different <u>scales</u>. It can be a <u>local scale</u>, e.g. a local radio station, a <u>national scale</u>, e.g. a national newspaper, or even a <u>global scale</u>, e.g. the World Wide Web. The larger the scale it operates on, the greater the <u>influence</u> it can have, as it can reach <u>more people</u>.

A Free Press is an Important Part of Democracy

1) In a <u>democratic</u> country like the UK, the media have the <u>right</u> to investigate and report on issues that are of interest to the public, without it being <u>strictly controlled</u> by the government.
2) This is called a <u>free press</u> — it means information is <u>uncensored</u> and people can express their opinions without interference from the government. It's a bit like <u>freedom of speech</u>.
3) This doesn't mean that the press can print <u>anything</u> they want to — there are some occasions when they <u>aren't allowed</u> to publish certain bits of information, usually to <u>protect</u> people (see next page).
4) In some countries there is <u>heavy censorship</u>. Articles are checked, usually by the government, before they're released to make sure they're saying what the government wants the public to read.
5) The problem with this is that it stops the public from knowing the whole <u>truth</u>. E.g. leading up to an election, a government might only let papers publish good things about themselves and bad things about the opposition — giving the public a <u>biased</u> version of events (see page 58).

Reporting Should be Accurate and Fair

1) The role of the media is often seen as keeping the public <u>informed</u> — so, many people think the media have a moral responsibility to write reports that are <u>fair</u>, and <u>factually correct</u>.
2) Sometimes stories intrude into people's <u>private lives</u>. Some people think this is unacceptable.
3) To make sure that reports are fair, accurate and respect people's privacy, there are <u>organisations</u> whose job is to <u>monitor</u> different elements of the media.

1) In the UK, there's a voluntary code of practice for the media that's managed by the <u>Press Complaints Commission</u> (PCC). Newspapers all agree to follow this code.

2) The PCC has a <u>Code of Practice Committee</u>, made up of newspaper and magazine editors. They deal with any complaints and make a judgement, which is then printed in the newspaper or magazine.

3) <u>OFCOM (Office of Communications)</u> produces guidelines for radio and television programme makers to follow. If someone complains, it has to decide if the programme has broken the rules.

4) Several other agencies keep an eye (or ear) on television and radio to make sure that they follow the guidelines. The <u>Advertising Standards Authority</u> checks that adverts don't mislead, or cause offence.

And the secret of life turned out to be CENSORED...

Nice easy start here — the UK has <u>freedom of the press</u>, so the media are <u>legally</u> allowed to report on pretty much what they want. But they have to report <u>fairly</u>, so there are organisations to check up on 'em.

Media Laws

Even though the UK media is mostly <u>self-regulated</u>, there are certain <u>laws</u> that they have to abide by and certain things that they're <u>not allowed</u> to report. And, surprise surprise, you need to know what they are.

Media Laws Restrict What the Media Can Report

1) Media laws protect the <u>rights</u> of the people being reported on by the media — they limit intrusion into people's private lives.

2) There are also laws to make sure media stories are fair and accurate. They try to stop lies being printed (<u>libel</u>) or broadcast (<u>slander</u>).

3) Other laws protect <u>vulnerable</u> groups of people from things that might be <u>offensive</u> or <u>unsuitable</u>, e.g. television programmes with adult content can only be shown after a certain time (the watershed).

4) It's also against the law to publish things that damage the chance of a <u>fair trial</u> in court, or that put the country in <u>danger</u> (e.g. publishing secret plans, or naming our spies).

5) Sometimes people's names aren't allowed to be printed, to <u>protect their identity</u> — e.g. children accused of serious crimes can't be named for legal reasons and the identities of people who <u>inform</u> the police about criminals are often protected for their own safety.

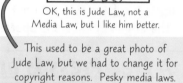

OK, this is Jude Law, not a Media Law, but I like him better.

This used to be a great photo of Jude Law, but we had to change it for copyright reasons. Pesky media laws.

There are Four Main Laws Affecting the Media (Each Has a Posh Title)

The media need to consider four laws when they're reporting something:

<u>Defamation law</u>	If a newspaper prints stuff about someone that isn't true, this is known as <u>libel</u>, and the person can sue for damages. E.g. the actress Cameron Diaz successfully sued the National Enquirer for incorrectly claiming that she had cheated on her boyfriend.
The <u>Obscene Publications Act</u>	It's a criminal offence for newspapers to print anything that's considered <u>obscene</u>, e.g. explicit photographs.
The <u>Official Secrets Act</u>	The government can stop things classed as <u>official secret</u> being printed, e.g. war plans. '<u>Gagging orders</u>' are used to ban the publication of the information.
<u>Contempt of Court</u>	The law can tell newspapers not to print certain information, e.g. if a press story might influence a <u>court case</u>. If they do print it they'll be held in contempt of court and be prosecuted.

There's also the <u>Human Rights Act</u> (see p.4) — this protects everyone's right to <u>respect for their privacy</u>. So things like taking and publishing embarrassing or humiliating photographs of someone may break this law.

Lisa sued the Daily Banana after they published photos of her in the nude.

What the Media Can Report Varies for Different Situations

1) If the media are <u>prosecuted</u> for breaking a media law and found guilty, they'll be punished.

2) Punishments vary depending on what they've done, but can include paying <u>compensation</u>, or issuing a <u>public apology</u>. If someone is responsible for printing something which is obscene or has been banned by the law, they can even be sent to <u>prison</u>. Blimey — best watch what I write then.

The media have to follow laws like the rest of us...

You often hear about people, especially famous people, <u>suing</u> the papers for printing lies or invading their privacy. If media laws didn't exist, the press could print any lies they liked, with nothing to stop them.

The Media and Politics

The media has a lot of <u>power</u>. It can influence what people think and what they do. A scary thought...

The Media Can Influence or Reflect Public Opinion

1) The media controls what people <u>see</u> and <u>hear</u> about goings-on in the world, which makes it very <u>powerful</u>.

2) <u>Which</u> issues capture the media's attention <u>influences public opinion</u>. For example, if the news is full of information about a famine in Africa, the public are likely to feel concerned about the people it affects. (There might be even worse suffering going on elsewhere but if the media isn't interested, few other people will be.)

3) <u>How</u> the media reports issues also influences public opinion. Media reports don't always present <u>just</u> the facts — they often include opinions, unfounded claims, theories or speculations. Some reports use <u>emotive language</u> and <u>visual images</u> to influence the public to feel a certain way. This is known as <u>bias</u> (see p. 58).

4) The media can also make people <u>think more carefully</u> about certain issues and <u>raise awareness</u> of them. For example, soaps like EastEnders can raise awareness about issues like drug addiction.

5) People are most likely to watch or buy media that has the <u>same point of view</u> as them, so it's important for media reports to <u>reflect the opinion</u> of the target audience if they want to make money.

The media often use questionnaires called <u>opinion polls</u> to find out what public opinion is. They can then report in a way that reflects this. So if a poll showed that most people were against a particular government policy, a newspaper might also take this stance.

The media creates rumours of a really bad smell near Milton Keynes.

The Media Can Have a Big Influence on Politics

The media can exert <u>pressure</u> on local and national governments to adopt particular policies by drawing attention to certain issues and influencing public opinion. For example:

- In 2008 the Daily Telegraph wanted the government to abandon plans to increase <u>fuel duty</u> and to stop a planned increase in <u>vehicle excise duty</u> (road tax). It thought the cost of driving was too high.
- It launched a "<u>Fair Deal for Drivers</u>" campaign in May 2008 to put pressure on the government.
- The campaign drew public attention to the planned increases and over 10 000 people signed a <u>petition</u> supporting it.

- Lorry drivers protested about the increases, holding <u>demonstrations</u>, <u>blocking roads</u> and <u>slowing traffic</u> across the country. Some former and current politicians <u>publicly supported</u> the newspaper's stance, as did several motoring organisations, e.g. the AA and the RAC.

- In July 2008 the government <u>postponed</u> the fuel duty increase from October 2008, until April 2009. Many people think the media campaign and the <u>public support</u> of it influenced this decision.

People Can Influence Public Opinion Using the Media

1) <u>Politicians</u> use the media to inform the public about their policies and to persuade people to vote for them.

2) Open <u>debates</u> and <u>discussion forums</u> on TV and radio programmes, <u>party political broadcasts</u> or newspaper articles that include in-depth <u>political discussion</u> can all help politicians to get their points of view across.

3) Politicians often use media that share their political views to 'champion' (support) their cause. By subtly pushing a political viewpoint, the media can have a big effect on the <u>popularity of political parties</u>. E.g. many people think The Sun's <u>favouritism</u> of New Labour contributed to its popularity in the 1990s.

4) It isn't just politicians that use the media to influence the public — other individuals and groups use it too. For example, pressure groups like Greenpeace and Fathers4Justice™ (see pages 15-16) often appear in the media, hoping to gain public <u>support</u> and encourage politicians to address the issues.

The media influences you whether you know it or not...

The power of the media is scarily huge. Don't assume that the media just <u>innocently</u> present facts for us to digest — they often have a hidden agenda to influence public opinion and cause <u>change</u>. Sneaky.

Fact, Opinion and Bias in the Media

Believe it or not, you can't always take everything the media says at <u>face value</u>. I know, who'd have guessed..

Reports May Contain Facts and Opinions

You need to be able to tell the difference between <u>facts</u> and <u>opinions</u> in media reports.

FACTS

Facts are <u>true statements</u> that don't depend on what someone thinks — they're <u>objective</u>.
For example, "Labour won the 2005 general election", "The Sun sells more copies than any other British newspaper" and "More pupils achieved 5 A*-C GCSE grades in 2009 than in 1999" are all facts.

OPINIONS

Opinions are just what people <u>think</u> — they're <u>subjective</u>.
For example, "Labour will win the next general election", "The Sun is the best newspaper" and "GCSEs are getting easier" are all opinions. Some people will <u>agree</u> with these statements but others <u>won't</u>.

Many Media Reports are Biased

1) Media laws stop the media from telling lies (see p. 56). They don't state that they have to tell the <u>whole story</u> though — so some media reports might be <u>biased</u>.

THE DAILY TRASH
SPONSORED BY
LARD-U-LIKE
NEW! The LARD-BURGER
NUTRITIOUS AND DELICIOUS!
The perfect start to your day...
Joke Police Over-worked and Stressed

- The simplest form of bias is just <u>not running</u> a story. E.g. a newspaper sponsored by a fast-food chain is unlikely to publish a story about burgers being bad for you.
- Reports can also be biased if stories are presented in a <u>certain way</u>. E.g. a news headline calling genetically-modified crops "Frankenstein foods".
- Reports may also use <u>emotive language</u> and <u>strong visual images</u> to influence public opinion. E.g. a news station using photos of injured children in a report about a war they consider wrong.

2) Bias often reflects the views of the newspaper's owner — and a paper will often support a <u>political party</u>.

3) The <u>broadcast media</u>, including the BBC, are <u>assumed</u> to be <u>impartial</u>. However, how news is <u>selected</u> and <u>presented</u> will always reflect some bias, so you should always look at a range of sources.

You Need to be Able to Identify Facts, Opinions and Bias

In the exam you could be asked to <u>identify</u> facts, opinions and bias in media reports, so you need to be able to tell the difference between them. The article below is a film review written for a local newspaper in Warrington.

FACT — these are <u>true</u> pieces of information about the film. They <u>don't vary</u> depending on a person's point of view

BIAS — the review is in a Warrington-based paper so could be biased to write <u>positively</u> about the area and the people who live there.

Gloop and Gunder, starring Julien Franco and Ryan Bloy, is a charming film that will delight young children and parents alike. Set in the North-West of England in the 1970s it tells the tale of Gloop the goblin, who is sent to live with a human family in Warrington. Here he meets Gunder, the family's youngest boy, and the two strike up an unlikely friendship. The screenplay is crisp and engaging and allows the humour and spirit unique to the people of Warrington to shine through. A must-see.

OPINION — some people might not agree with these statements. They might have <u>different points of view</u>.

Gunder's opinion was that Gloop's polka-dot scarf only made him look sillier.

Bias is the most difficult one to identify — you might have to look at what the source is, who wrote it and whether there's any reason for them to be biased.

One more fact for you — you need to learn this page...

Knowing what facts, opinions and bias are is important (<u>fact</u>). And also interesting (<u>opinion</u>). But you'll have no probs, as this page is beautifully written, wonderfully presented and practically perfect in every way (<u>bias</u>).

Quick Test

Ah, the media and democracy, where would we be without them... No soaps, no trashy magazines, no email. It doesn't bear thinking about. And democracy's pretty good too I s'pose.

Anyway, you need to make sure that you know all the facts and explanations that have been so nicely laid out for you in this section. It's only a tiddly little section, so there aren't too many nasty facts and explanations to get your head around. And to help you out even more, here are some lovely questions so that you can check that you know your stuff. I know, I know, I'm too kind...

1) Describe the three main types of media.

2) What is a free press?

3) Explain why censorship of the press is undemocratic.

4) Briefly describe the purpose of the Code of Practice Committee of the PCC.

5) Name the organisation that is responsible for checking that adverts aren't misleading.

6) Why does the media have to follow media guidelines? Give more than one reason.

7) What is the difference between 'libel' and 'slander'?

8) Sometimes the press aren't allowed to print certain information, in order to protect someone's identity. Give two situations where this might be the case.

9) Explain what the following laws are responsible for controlling:
   a) Defamation law   b) The Official Secrets Act   c) Contempt of Court

10) What is a gagging order?

11) Explain why the media is able to influence public opinion.

12) Why do media reports need to reflect public opinion?

13) What is an opinion poll?

14) Describe one situation where the press have influenced government policy.

15) Give three ways that politicians can use the media to communicate their points of view to the public.

16) Give an example of a group (other than a political party) that use the media to influence public opinion.

17) Explain the difference between a fact and an opinion.

18) Identify the following statements as facts or opinions:
   a) Pizza is delicious.
   b) London is the capital of England.
   c) Manchester is great.
   d) Monday morning is the most depressing time of the week.
   e) Maths is taught in British schools.

19) Media reports can be biased. Describe two forms of bias.

The UK and Europe

In 1997 you became a citizen of Europe. Best understand what that means then...

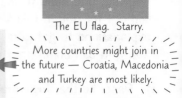

The EU flag. Starry.

The European Union is Growing

1) The European Union (EU) has 27 member countries at the moment:

   • France, Germany, Belgium, The Netherlands, Luxembourg, Italy, Spain, Portugal, UK, Ireland, Denmark, Greece, Sweden, Finland and Austria joined before 2004.

   • Since then the EU has admitted Cyprus, the Czech Republic, Estonia, Hungary, Latvia, Lithuania, Malta, Poland, Slovakia, Slovenia, Bulgaria and Romania.

   More countries might join in the future — Croatia, Macedonia and Turkey are most likely.

2) The member countries agree to work together, obey EU laws and contribute money to the EU budget.

The EU Government is a Complicated Organisation

1) EU countries share laws about things like human rights and follow rules about things like fishing and farming

2) The EU government is complicated. Here's how EU decisions get made:

European Commission		European Parliament		Council of the European Union	
27 members — appointed by the governments of the member countries.	Drafts new laws on economic, social and foreign policy. Members can be questioned and their decisions blocked by the Parliament.	736 members (MEPs) — directly elected by EU citizens.	Debates and amends laws proposed by the Commission. Controls the EU budget along with the Council.	Made up of one minister from the government of each member country.	Must agree with the Parliament on amendments to new laws.

Once policies have been approved by the Parliament and the Council they are passed back to the Commission to implement.

3) The European Court of Justice and the European Court of Human Rights interpret EU laws — they can overrule the decisions of national courts. EU citizens can appeal to the European courts for a judgement.

The European Union is a Single Market

1) EU countries trade between themselves without tariffs. Tariffs are charges a country imposes on goods imported from abroad. This 'single market' means businesses have a huge number of people to sell their goods to — which can boost economies and create jobs. However, some small businesses have found it hard to compete.

2) EU citizens are allowed to live, work, study, and get healthcare and social welfare in any EU country.

3) EU membership brings other benefits too. E.g. environmental laws are more effective, consumer rights laws are the same across all EU countries, and fighting international crime and illegal immigration is easier.

4) Some people reckon that being part of the EU is good because it helps keep the peace in Europe, as well as giving countries a bigger say in world events.

Not Everyone Agrees with the EU Government

1) A lot of people in this country have problems with the EU government:

   • The European Parliament has a reputation as a 'talking shop' that doesn't actually achieve much, e.g. saying that bananas mustn't be too bent, that sort of thing.

   • The European Commission is sometimes seen as undemocratic, because its members are appointed, not elected — some people don't like the idea that laws and economic decisions get made by people we haven't voted for.

   • Some people are concerned that the UK's given up too much independence, or that the member countries are too diverse for the EU to be effective.

   • Free trade campaigners criticise the single market for imposing tariffs on poor countries outside the EU.

2) Big decisions have good and bad sides, e.g. the Common Agricultural Policy, which guarantees prices for farmers' produce, meant that too much of some things were made ('wine lakes' and 'butter mountains').

Fog in channel — Continent cut off...

...as the joke about the old British newspaper headline goes. We're not so cut off these days though, and not just 'cos of the Channel Tunnel. You need to know about the pros and cons of being part of the EU.

The Commonwealth

The British Empire was the name for all the countries around the world that were ruled by Britain. By the end of the 19th century the British Empire included about a quarter of the Earth's population, but after World War II the colonies started to become independent. The days of the Empire are long gone — but it was the foundation of the Commonwealth of Nations.

The British Empire Became the Commonwealth

1) Nearly all the members of the Commonwealth of Nations are former British colonies. After they gained independence they chose to join the Commonwealth (once called the British Commonwealth of Nations).

2) There are now 54 members of the Commonwealth of Nations. The British monarch is still its official Head (she's also the monarch of 15 other countries, including Canada, Jamaica and Australia).

3) The Commonwealth is mainly a forum for discussion. Heads of each country meet every two years to discuss things that concern all members — like human rights issues, economic and social development, and the environment.

Commonwealth countries.

4) Its principles are outlined in the Harare Declaration (1991). They're basically:
   - International peace and the rule of international law.
   - Democracy and equal rights for all.
   - Opposition to racism and racial oppression.
   - Economic development to improve living standards in poor countries.

Countries that don't promote these principles aren't allowed to be members, e.g. South Africa couldn't be a member from 1961-1994, because its policy of apartheid treated Black South Africans very badly (see page 5).

Members can be Suspended from the Commonwealth

1) In 1995, the Commonwealth Ministerial Action Group was set up. This group has the power to discipline governments that go against the Commonwealth's principles.

2) In March 2002, Zimbabwe was suspended from the Commonwealth after reports of intimidation and vote-rigging by the ZANU-PF party during the country's elections. Zimbabwe withdrew from the Commonwealth in 2003.

3) Apart from suspension, the Commonwealth doesn't have any real power. It doesn't act as a single political entity, or have any influence over non-member countries.

The Commonwealth Flag. Sunny.

The Commonwealth Promotes Cultural Understanding

Is one nearly there yet?

It's just round the corner ma'am.

The Queen at the Commonwealth Games.

1) The Commonwealth was originally about trade agreements and defence, but these links have become less important. Cultural and sporting links still are important, though.

2) The Commonwealth Games is held every four years. It's known as the Friendly Games and aims to improve relations between Commonwealth countries.

3) It's a competition including lots of sports, like athletics, swimming, gymnastics, rugby sevens and netball.

4) In 1987 the Commonwealth Writers' Prize was set up to encourage new writers, and make sure good books were read outside the country they came from.

Monopoly is my favourite Common Wealth Game...

Whether you think the British Empire was a good thing or a bad thing, it changed the face of the world. Make sure you understand how the Commonwealth came about, and what it actually means today.

The United Nations

The <u>United Nations</u> was formed after World War II to try to stop wars. <u>Nearly every country</u> is a member.

The UN Tries to *Resolve Conflicts* and *Protect Victims*

1) The UN's <u>192 member countries</u> all signed the UN charter agreeing to:
    - resolve disputes <u>peacefully</u> and prevent acts of <u>aggression</u>.
    - respect <u>international laws</u> and protect <u>human rights</u>. ➡ *The <u>Universal Declaration of Human Rights</u> says that UN members agree to protect everyone's <u>right</u> to <u>life</u> and to <u>freedom</u> from things like <u>slavery</u>, <u>torture</u>, <u>discrimination</u>, and <u>unfair trials</u> (see pages 3-6 for more on human rights).*
    - <u>cooperate</u> to solve international <u>economic</u>, <u>social</u> and <u>humanitarian problems</u> (e.g. famines).

2) The <u>General Assembly</u> is an annual meeting of representatives of <u>all</u> UN members. One of its jobs is to vote on <u>General Assembly resolutions</u>, e.g. condemning killings in Bosnia in 1993. Resolutions are only <u>recommendations</u>, but show a strong <u>international opinion</u>.

3) The UN's <u>international court</u> (The International Court of Justice) rules on <u>international disagreements</u>, e.g. disputes about where borders lie.

4) The UN set the ball rolling to establish an independent International Criminal Court. This was set up in 2002 to <u>prosecute people</u> accused of breaking humanitarian laws (e.g. committing <u>war crimes</u> or <u>genocide</u>).
    - <u>Genocide</u> is killing a large number of the members of a national, racial, religious or ethnic group, e.g. the killing of Jews in World War II, or of Bosnian Muslims in 1995.
    - <u>War crimes</u> include <u>mistreating prisoners of war</u>, <u>killing children</u> or <u>civilians</u> that get caught up in fighting, and unnecessarily <u>destroying property</u>.

The UN flag. Leafy.

The UN *Security Council* Discusses *Peace and Security*

1) The <u>Security Council</u> has 15 member countries. If a country acts aggressively, the Security Council can pass <u>Security Council Resolutions</u> — allowing the UN to impose <u>economic sanctions</u> (stop people trading with them), or take <u>military action</u>. After a conflict, the UN will often send in <u>peacekeeping troops</u> to help make sure peace agreements are kept to.

2) Since the 1990s, <u>British</u> forces have had big peacekeeping roles in <u>Sierra Leone</u>, <u>Bosnia</u> and <u>Kosovo</u>.

> **SECURITY COUNCIL MEMBERS**
>
> The Security Council has five <u>permanent</u> member countries (the victors of World War II — the <u>USA</u>, the <u>UK</u>, <u>France</u>, <u>China</u> and <u>Russia</u>), and ten elected members that <u>change</u> every two years. The permanent members have the power to <u>veto</u> a resolution — they can <u>stop</u> a resolution even if <u>all</u> the other countries <u>agree</u> to it.
>
> Because of this, countries like Brazil, Germany, India, and Japan think they should be <u>permanent members</u> too — but not enough countries <u>agree</u> who should join the original five.

The *Kyoto Protocol* is an Agreement to *Pollute Less*

1) The <u>Kyoto Protocol</u> is a UN agreement signed in Kyoto, Japan in 1997, to try to stop <u>climate change</u> from getting too bad (see page 26). By 2005, enough countries had signed up to make it <u>legally binding</u>.

2) Industrialised countries were set targets to reduce their <u>greenhouse gas</u> emissions.

> The UK's <u>on track</u> to reduce greenhouse gas emissions to <u>12.5% lower than 1990 levels</u> by 2012 (as long as you don't count the emissions in other countries due to our imports).
> - Switching from <u>coal</u> to <u>oil and gas</u> power stations means <u>less CO_2</u> is produced.
> - More <u>recycling</u> means there's <u>less methane</u> coming out of <u>landfill sites</u>.
> - Better <u>nylon manufacture</u> and less <u>fertiliser use</u> means <u>less nitrous oxide</u> is produced by industry and farms.

Kyoto — not just an anagram of Tokyo and OK toy...

You need to know how international agreements affect the UK — so don't forget we've signed UN agreements on human rights and the Kyoto protocol, and that British troops take part in peacekeeping around the world.

The United Nations, G8 and NATO

You need to know about the UN's Millennium Development Goals, and also about a couple of other international organisations — the G8 (an economic council), and NATO (a defence alliance).

The Millennium Development Goals Aim to Help the Poor

Eight Millennium Goals were agreed by UN members in 2000. They all aim to improve the standard of living in poorer countries. All member countries agreed to try and achieve them by 2015 — poorer countries promised to improve the way their countries are run, and wealthy countries promised to provide the resources to help them make the changes. The goals include these targets:

1) Reduce by half those suffering from hunger and poverty.
2) Make sure all children get primary education.
3) Make sure girls get as much education as boys.
4) Reduce by two-thirds the death rate of children under 5.
5) Reduce by three-quarters the death rate of mothers in childbirth.
6) Stop the spread of HIV/AIDS.
7) Improve environmental sustainability (see p. 27) and halve the proportion of people without sustainable access to safe drinking water).
8) Have an open trading and financial system that doesn't make it hard for less developed countries to trade.

Countries like China are close to meeting these goals, but many African countries are not.

The G8 is a meeting of Eight Rich Countries

1) The G8 members are the United States, the UK, Germany, France, Italy, Japan, Canada and Russia.
2) The heads of government of the G8 members meet every year to discuss world economic problems.
3) They met in 2008 and 2009 to cooperate to deal with the financial crisis (caused by banks lending money to people who couldn't afford to pay it back), and to try to stop it happening again.
4) The G8 will be replaced by the G20 in the future as the main economic meeting. The G20 includes more African, South American and Asian countries, as well as heads of international banks.
5) There are often big protests at the same time as these summits — people blame the leaders for not doing enough to sort out things like poverty in Africa, global warming and HIV/AIDS.

Members of NATO agree to Defend Each Other

1) NATO stands for North Atlantic Treaty Organisation. It has 28 members including Britain, the USA, France and Germany.
2) NATO is the world's most powerful defence alliance. Article 5 of the treaty basically says:

   "An attack on one member is considered an attack on the entire alliance".

3) NATO was set up by the USA and countries in Western Europe when there was a lot of tension between these countries and the Communist East of Europe. Now three former communist countries (Poland, Hungary and the Czech Republic) are members of NATO.
4) NATO's first military action was in the former Yugoslavia in the early '90s. This was a peacekeeping mission, to try and help limit the bloodshed caused by the civil war in Yugoslavia.

The NATO flag. Pointy.

Would you like to join NATO — No Ta...
The UK's part of so many international organisations, that even my head's spinning. Just make sure that you don't get your UN mixed up with your NATO, or your Commonwealth with your G8, and it'll all be OK.

International Conflict

The war in Afghanistan is a very difficult issue. It shows that international diplomacy doesn't always work.

Relations with Afghanistan Broke Down after Bombings

1) In 1996 the Taliban, a religious and political group, seized control of most of Afghanistan after years of civil war. They were only recognised as legitimate rulers by three countries.

2) In 1998, a group supported by the Taliban and led by Osama bin Laden bombed US embassies in Tanzania and Kenya, killing over 200 people.

3) The UN imposed financial sanctions on Afghanistan in 1999 and 2000 (blocking the Taliban's access to their foreign bank accounts) to try to make them hand over Osama bin Laden for trial.

The September 11 attacks led to War

1) On 11th September 2001, terrorist attacks in the USA killed nearly 3000 people and destroyed the World Trade Centre.

2) On 12th September, NATO invoked Article 5 of its charter for the first time in its history (see p. 63). The attack on the USA was treated as an attack on the whole alliance, so Canada and most of Europe were expected to support the USA.

3) The USA found evidence that Al-Qaeda (a Taliban-supported group led by Osama bin Laden) were responsible for the attacks. The US president demanded that the Taliban hand over Al-Qaeda leaders and close terrorist training camps, and declared a "war on terror". A Taliban offer to try Osama bin Laden in Afghanistan was rejected.

4) On October 7, 2001, the US and UK started to help anti-Taliban Afghan forces overthrow the Taliban. They sent in soldiers and started bombing raids. They also sent aid, including food and medical supplies, to the civilian population. Millions were facing starvation because the fighting disrupted food supplies.

The Taliban Lost Power but Kept Up Insurgent Attacks

1) After a series of battles with Afghan and NATO troops, Taliban troops were forced out of Kabul, and then out of their last stronghold, Kandahar, in December 2001. Osama bin Laden escaped to Pakistan.

2) The UN Security Council (p. 62) arranged meetings between other Afghan leaders. They set up a temporary government. UN peacekeepers (p. 62) arrived to help control the capital.

3) From 2003 onwards, a Taliban insurgency (rebellion) began. This meant increased attacks on Afghan and foreign soldiers by small groups of Taliban fighters, often with roadside bombs.

4) In 2005, despite Taliban attempts to disrupt them, elections were held and an Afghan parliament was set up. However, the new government had little control outside Kabul, and was criticised for corruption.

More Troops Were Needed to Help the Afghan Forces

1) Taliban attacks and problems with illegal drug production worsened between 2006 and 2009.

2) More US and NATO troops arrived, especially in 2008 and 2009, to improve security and train the Afghan army and police to eventually take control of the country.

3) By the end of 2009 there were over 64 000 US and NATO troops in Afghanistan. Over 1000 NATO troops had been killed, including over 230 British soldiers.

4) A large number of US and UK citizens are strongly against the war. However, studies suggest most Afghans think it is good that the Taliban were removed. Aid programmes mean more people now have access to electricity, immunisation and education than in 2001.

War against Terrorism or War of Aggression...

Should we bring our troops home straight away? But if we did that, and Afghanistan descended into chaos, would that be worse? Whatever you think, make sure you can discuss how effective sanctions, force and aid have been.

Quick Test

International bodies like the EU and UN might seem distant from your daily life, but lots of things we take for granted (like international peace and trade) do depend on them working properly. Of course, what we can't take for granted is that you've got all the useful facts about them nicely filed away for future reference — so what better than a nice little revision summary to check it's all sunk in?

1) How many countries are members of the EU?

2) Which part of the European government is directly elected by EU citizens?

3) Which part of European government has the final say on EU decisions?

4) What is the main financial benefit to countries of being a member of the EU?

5) What rights do you have as a European citizen in EU countries?

6) Give one argument that often gets raised against the European Commission.

7) Give a good and a bad side of the Common Agricultural Policy.

8) What is the Commonwealth of Nations?

9) State <u>three</u> principles of the Commonwealth of Nations.

10) How often do the Commonwealth Heads of Government meet?
   Do they:
   a) Think up ideas for new reality TV shows?
   b) Discuss important issues that affect all the members?
   c) Hold a wide range of sporting contests?

11) What is the strongest action that the Commonwealth can take against its members?

12) Name two Commonwealth competitions that promote cultural understanding.

13) What is the UN's main purpose?

14) How many countries have signed up to the UN Declaration of Human Rights?
   a) 27   b) 192   c) 53

15) Name some of the rights that the UN Declaration of Human Rights protects.

16) What is genocide?

17) What is the purpose of the International Criminal Court?

18) What are UN peacekeepers?

19) How do the USA, the UK, France, China and Russia differ from other Security Council members?

20) What is the Kyoto Protocol?

21) What has the UK done to help meet the conditions of the Kyoto Protocol?

22) Name three of the UN's Millennium Development Goals.

23) What is the difference between the way that poor and wealthy countries contribute to achieving the Millennium Development Goals?

24) What do the G8 countries meet to discuss?

25) Why was NATO originally set up?

26) Why did the USA originally want to prosecute Osama bin Laden?
   What measures did they use to try and bring him to trial?

27) What measures did the USA and UK use to remove the Taliban?
   How well did these measures work?

28) How did the Taliban fight back after they had been removed from power?

29) What are the two main roles of the US and NATO troops in Afghanistan?

30) How have conditions improved in Afghanistan since 2001?

Researching Your Project

For this part of Citizenship, you get to research an issue and do something about it.

The Project is Worth 60% of the Short Course GCSE

1) You have to look into a Citizenship issue and put together an argument to get your point of view across.

2) Next you have to plan and take part in some type of action, then evaluate the impact your action has had.

3) You can work in a group for the research and action stages. But you'll have to do the writing up by yourself.

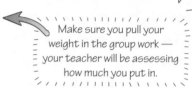

Make sure you pull your weight in the group work — your teacher will be assessing how much you put in.

4) Your teacher will give you as much help as they're allowed to by the exam board, so do ask them... but mostly it's up to you to make a good job of your project.

The exact details of your project depend on which exam board you're following — but the tips on these pages are relevant to them all.

First You Need to Decide on Your Issue

1) You might be allowed to choose your own issue, or your teacher might give you one.

2) Your issue must relate to a Citizenship topic covered in this book. Some examples of issues are:

> **Should schools try to use less energy?**
> (this relates to the 'Sustainable development' content area)

> **Should young offenders face harsher punishments?**
> (this ties in to the 'Law and justice' content area)

3) If you are allowed to choose your own issue, pick one that bothers you — that way you'll be motivated to make your campaign really good.

Your Research is Really Important

The research you do depends on your issue — but here are some examples of stuff it might be useful find out.

1) Look at the facts, like what the law says, how long it's been like that and why it's like that.
E.g. the minimum wage became law in 1999 to prevent workers from being underpaid, but it doesn't apply to people of compulsory school age.

2) Try to find statistics about the issue, e.g. how many people would be affected if your campaign succeeds?
E.g. you could find out how many people in your school have a part-time job and how much they get paid.

3) Find out what other people think. Don't just ask your mates — talk to teachers, parents, local employers and even your local MP. By asking a wide range of people you're likely to get both sides of the argument.

A questionnaire might be a good way to collect this information.

E.g. some people might think it's unfair that under-16s aren't paid the minimum wage if they do the same job as someone older. But some people might think that this would only encourage children to work instead of focusing on their education.

But there are some things to watch out for when doing your research — see the next page.

4) The internet's dead useful — e.g. you can find out the law in other countries, search for relevant newspaper articles, read online blogs...
E.g. in some US states, the minimum wage does apply to under-16s.

5) Interview people in positions of power (see next page).

6) Collect evidence of your research as you go.
E.g. keep filled-in questionnaires, newspaper cuttings or printouts from websites.
Make a recording of any interviews you do (ask the interviewee's permission first though).

More on Researching Your Project

Be careful when you're doing your research — you can't take everything the media says at face value.

Reports May Contain Facts and Opinions

You need to be able to identify facts and opinions when doing your research, as well as spotting bias. Here's a quick reminder of what's what:

FACTS Facts are true statements that don't depend on what someone thinks — they're objective. For example, "The minimum wage for 16-year-olds in 2009/10 was £3.57 per hour", and "40% of 15-year-olds have a regular part-time job" are both facts.

OPINIONS Opinions are what people think — they're subjective. For example, "Young people should focus on their school work rather than a job", and "It's not fair that young people are paid less than older people" are both opinions. Some people will agree with these statements but others won't.

BIAS Some media reports can be biased — they might not tell the whole story, or present facts in a way that supports their opinion. Make sure you always check more than one source.

See page 58 for more on bias.

Stuff on Citizenship Issues Goes Out of Date Quickly

1) Citizenship isn't like History. The Battle of Hastings took place in 1066 — that'll never change. But laws and policies do change. E.g. it wasn't very long ago that 16-year-olds could buy cigarettes.

2) And, as time goes by, society changes. If you found some statistics on youth employment in 1980, they'd probably not tell you much about today — so always check the dates of your sources.

You Could Talk to People in Positions of Power

Communicating with people in positions of power, e.g. your local MP or school governors, is always sensible if you hope to get something changed (and your exam board might tell you to do this). Remember:

- Make sure that the people you choose could have some effect on the issue you're looking at.

  E.g. talking to the Arctic Monkeys might be fun, but shorter jail sentences for young offenders probably isn't their area.

- If you're looking at an issue that affects your school, you need to talk to your headteacher.
- But if your issue involves the local community, it'll be your local councillors or MP who you should talk to.

  E.g. you'd have to communicate with your local MP to try to get the government to lower the age at which the national minimum wage is paid.

- Be realistic — the Prime Minister might be the ideal person to talk to, but he's a bit busy. Your local MP's probably a better bet.
- Make sure you go prepared — do your research so you know all the facts. Have a list of questions you want to ask, and try not to leave until you've got the answers.

Don't forget to get some evidence of your interviews — e.g. a witness statement or a DVD/tape recording.

Decide What Your Research Shows

1) Once you've done all your research and interviews, you need to come up with a balanced argument.
2) It's important that you look at both sides of the issue — otherwise your argument could be biased.
3) You need to understand and explain why people have particular views on your issue to get good marks.

Is Superman in a position of power?...

Make sure you look out for facts, opinions and bias in the sources you use — it'll help you make a balanced argument. Use a wide range of sources to get different points of view on both sides of the issue.

Planning Your Action

Learn to walk before you run... or in Citizenship speak, learn to plan your action before you carry it out.

Spend Time Planning What Action You're Going to Take

1) If you're working in a group, work together to plan what action you're going to take.

2) Make sure you're really clear about what you're trying to achieve and how you're going to achieve it.

3) You might want to promote your campaign within your school, or you might want to take it into the local community — check it's OK with your teacher first.

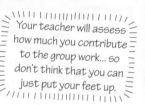

Your teacher will assess how much you contribute to the group work... so don't think that you can just put your feet up.

4) You have to be able to present your argument to the audience you want to reach. This doesn't just mean standing up and talking about it though. You could...

- organise a meeting to put your views across, e.g. to the school council, the headteacher or your local council
- develop a presentation about your issue and show it to other people
- set up a website or write a newspaper article for your local paper
- create posters and put up a display about your issue in your school, or ask your council if you can put it up at their offices or on noticeboards around town
- set up an action group and encourage people to join — then you can campaign together
- make leaflets, T-shirts or badges that highlight the issue

Make use of the skills each group member has. E.g. if someone's a great artist, maybe they could design a poster.

Share Out the Work Fairly

1) Make a detailed list of everything that needs doing for your campaign, then share out the activities (assuming you're working in a group).

2) Decide on deadlines for each task. It'd be sensible to get some things done first — e.g. if you're writing a letter to a busy person, get it in the post quick-smart — they might take a few weeks to reply.

3) It's a good idea to record what your group decides in a table like this (the exam board might provide one):

Group Member	Action	Deadline	Extra information
Sarah Smith	E-mail Mr Harris to arrange meeting.	21st March	Try to arrange meeting in early April.
Marco Polo	Design leaflet to give to all pupils.	1st April	Use computer to help design it.

4) You get marks for how well you work in a group — if the teacher sees you all squabbling, your marks will nosedive. On the other hand, if your group is sitting round not getting started, then taking the lead yourself would be a good thing to do.

Don't Expect Your Action to Run Perfectly

1) It's likely you'll need to make changes to your action plan along the way — it happens. For example, you might not be able to get an interview with the person you want to talk to, so you'd have to change your plan to take this into account.

2) Keep communicating with your team so that you all know what's going on and what needs to be changed.

3) You're likely to get marks for how well you deal with obstacles and solve problems, so don't panic.

Lights, camera, a lot of careful planning — ACTION...

You need to show good teamwork and individual skills to pick up full marks here. So remember to work together, listen to others and take the lead when necessary. And do your bit in the campaign really well. And above all... you can't expect your campaign to run smoothly if you don't put in the planning legwork.

Evaluating the Impact

When you've finished being active, it's time to put your feet up and have a <u>packet of crisps</u>.
Oh no it's not (sorry) — first you have to <u>evaluate</u> it. Then you can have a packet of crisps.

You Need Evidence of Your Action

Collect <u>evidence</u> as you go along of what you and your team get up to — it's not enough for you to just <u>describe</u> it. Here are some <u>examples</u> of different ways to gather evidence:

- <u>Save a copy</u> of anything you make like leaflets, posters or T-shirts.
- <u>Take photos</u> of any events or displays you do.
- <u>Record</u> or <u>video</u> any meetings you go to (as long as you have permission), as well as taking notes.
- Get <u>witness statements</u> from people who <u>observed</u> your action and saw what you did,
  e.g. your <u>teacher</u> might have been watching what you were up to.
- Get <u>witness statements</u> from people who are <u>influenced</u> by your action, e.g. your <u>headteacher</u>.

You Have to Assess the Impact of Your Action...

1) You need to think about the <u>impact</u> your action has on the <u>issue</u> you chose — did it <u>raise awareness</u>, <u>influence people</u> or get <u>changes</u> made? Did you <u>achieve</u> what you set out to do?

2) You need to measure the success of your action somehow.
   For example,

   - Give a <u>questionnaire</u> to people who see your display, or who attend your meeting or charity event — you can find out if people are now <u>more aware</u> of the issue, and what they thought of your action.
   - If you handed a <u>petition</u> to your local council, or put your views forward at a meeting, ask if they're planning to <u>change</u> anything as a result (or even just call another meeting about it).

...and Evaluate What You Did

1) Mention any <u>problems</u> you came across — and how you <u>solved</u> them.
   If your plan changed, then explain why.

2) Explain what you've <u>learnt</u> and what you'd do differently next time.

When you're writing things up, take care with your spelling, grammar and punctuation — or you'll lose marks.

The level of support for your project may surprise you.

3) Evaluate how well <u>your group</u> worked together, and how well <u>you</u> contributed.

4) Describe what your <u>next steps</u> would be if you (or someone else) were to take your action further, and the <u>impact</u> you think this would have.

5) Describe how your <u>own views</u> on the issue have changed during the project.

6) You have to link what you've done to the bigger, <u>national picture</u> — it might be that your action in the <u>local community</u> relates to a government policy or national campaign.

   E.g. if your issue involved increasing awareness of the range of religious beliefs in the community, it'd further the government's initiatives to promote community cohesion.

It went well — Mr Obama said he really liked my idea...

Whether you managed to change the world or not, you need to explain what you did, how it went and how it could have gone better. Remember to back up your statements with <u>evidence</u>, e.g. "As the letter shows, the local councillors support our campaign that less homework would definitely be better for our health".

The Controlled Assessment

Do Well in Your Exam

You've learnt all the <u>facts</u> — now it's time to get those <u>grades</u>.

The <u>Basics</u> — <u>Read</u> <u>the Questions</u>

The exam will be split into two or three sections.

1) <u>Read</u> the questions <u>carefully</u>.

2) The more <u>marks</u> a question's worth, the <u>longer</u> you should be spending on it.

3) Be aware of how much <u>time</u> you're using. You're told how much time you should spend on each section — take notice of it, or you mightn't have enough time for the last questions.

4) You should answer <u>all</u> the questions in the first section. In later sections you <u>might</u> get a <u>choice</u> of questions to answer (depending on your exam board) — so read each section carefully.

That's spelling, grammar, punctuation, and how clearly you express yourself.

5) One of the questions towards the end of the exam will assess the <u>quality</u> of your <u>written communication</u> — so use your best English when you write your answer.

There are <u>Easy Marks</u> <u>for Knowing What Things</u> <u>Mean</u>

1) Citizenship terms often have really <u>complicated meanings</u>, making these questions <u>trickier</u> than they look.

2) Questions about what terms mean are sometimes multiple choice. For example:

Clearly show your answer — it'll tell you how on the paper (e.g. circle the number or put a cross in the box).

What is the best description of a **bill**?
(i) A policy of a political party.
(ii) A civil law.
((iii)) A draft of a law.
(iv) A document listing human rights. **[1]**

Don't jump to conclusions — read <u>all</u> the possible answers and pick the <u>best one</u>.

It's always worth <u>guessing</u> multiple choice questions if you're not sure of the answer — you never know, you might just guess lucky.

3) Other short answer questions test what you know in a nice, straightforward way.

Even if you know more ways, you won't get extra marks for listing them — it's only a 1-mark question.

State **one** way that membership of the European Union affects UK citizens.
It means they can go and work in any other EU country. **[1]**

And <u>Marks</u> <u>for</u> <u>Explaining</u> <u>or</u> <u>Identifying</u> <u>Stuff</u>

Learn all the terms from the <u>glossary</u> — they'll be really useful for these questions.

1) Sometimes you need to write a bit more of an <u>explanation</u> of what a Citizenship term means...

Explain what is meant by the term 'community cohesion'.
The integration of a community through the mutual respect, understanding and actions of its members. **[2]**

The number of marks indicates how much you need to write — so add a bit more detail to get that second mark.

2) ... or you might need to give some <u>examples</u>.

Identify **two** ways in which a local council could promote sustainable development in the community.
1. Provide residents with recycling bins and make recycling collections.
2. Improve public transport, e.g. provide more bus services. **[2]**

Jock was unable to express his detailed knowledge of Citizenship issues — he couldn't get a grip on a pen with his flippers.

Do Well in Your Exam

After the one- and two-markers, the questions start to get a little bit <u>harder</u>...

You Might Have to Study Some Sources

1) Chances are, you'll be given some <u>sources</u> to read and then be asked <u>questions</u> relating to them.

2) Some questions can be answered <u>just</u> from the source, but most marks will come from using your <u>Citizenship knowledge</u>. For example:

---

1 Study Source A below.

> Source A: Newspaper report from the Chipperwell Green Gazette
>
> **Released murderer gets the holiday of a lifetime on the taxpayer**
> In 1995, Billy Jones brutally murdered his school friend in an act that will never be forgotten by the residents of Chipperwell Green. After serving just 15 years of a life sentence (much of which was spent on Easy Street in a youth prison), he is set to be released in March with a brand new identity and a comfortable life awaiting him in Hawaii — all paid for by the taxpayer.

(a) Identify **two** pieces of evidence from Source A which suggest that the report is biased.

1. The report is published by the Chipperwell Green Gazette — the local paper of the town
    where the murder happened, so the report is likely to be biased against the murderer.

2. The writer calls youth prison "Easy Street", which suggests they believe that youth prison
    isn't sufficient punishment for a murderer.   **[2]**

See p58 for stuff on bias.

(b) Which of the statements below is based purely on fact and not on bias or opinion?

- ☐ **A** Billy Jones brutally murdered his school friend.
- ☐ **B** The murder will never be forgotten by Chipperwell Green residents.
- ☒ **C** Billy Jones served 15 years in prison.
- ☐ **D** Billy Jones has a comfortable life awaiting him. **[1]**

The other answers are partly based on fact but are opinions too.

(c) Other than prison, state **two** other types of punishment used by the criminal justice service.

1. A fine.
2. Community service.   **[2]**

State means just give a short answer.

(d) Explain the factors that often contribute to ex-prisoners reoffending.

They have been with other criminals in prison, which can influence them to reoffend.
They often lose their jobs and contact with their families. This makes it difficult for
them to reintegrate back into society, and so more likely to reoffend.   **[2]**

Explain your reasoning to get full marks.

How to fail your Citizenship exam #49 — answer in hieroglyphics...

If you don't know the answer to a question, don't spend too much time pondering it. Get on with the other questions, and go back to the one you're stuck on later — you might have had a flash of inspiration by then.

Do Well in Your Exam

More stuff on the <u>exam</u> right here. Get <u>stuck in</u>.

You Could be Asked for Advice About a Problem

You might be given a <u>situation</u> and asked to give someone the <u>correct advice</u>. For example:

> Mark buys a toaster but finds out that it does not work. He takes it back to the shop with the receipt, but they explain that they can't replace it as they do not stock toasters any more, and they can't refund him as it was purchased five weeks ago. They tell him there is nothing they can do to help.

Study each of the alternative pieces of advice below.

(i) He can't get his money back. Tell him to just buy a toaster from a different shop.

(ii) His consumer rights say that he must be refunded, or the toaster repaired or replaced. Tell him to contact the Citizens' Advice Bureau.

(iii) His human rights say that he must be treated fairly. Tell him to contact the police.

Don't forget to circle the correct answer.

Evaluate the case and explain what advice you would give to Mark. In your answer you should:

• State clearly what your advice would be by putting a ring around alternatives i, ii, or iii above.

• Describe Mark's rights and the shopkeeper's responsibilities in this case.

• Evaluate the case and explain the reasons for your choice of alternative. **[4]**

State the <u>responsibility</u> and <u>right</u> in this case.

The business is responsible for providing goods of an acceptable standard. The Sale of Goods Act 1979 says that the consumer has the right to return faulty goods within six months and get a full refund, a replacement, or the item repaired. If the shop won't do one of these things, they are in breach of the contract of sale they made.

Back up your answer with <u>relevant</u> facts.

However, Mark doesn't need to contact the police because it is a civil offence, not a criminal offence. The Citizens' Advice Bureau provide free advice on consumer rights and will be able to help him.

Explain your reasoning.

You Might Have to Analyse Some Data

You might be given some <u>data</u> and asked to <u>analyse</u> it and <u>draw conclusions</u>. For example:

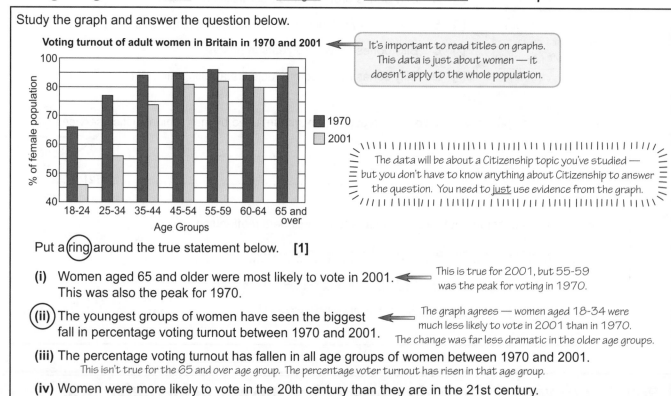

Study the graph and answer the question below.

Voting turnout of adult women in Britain in 1970 and 2001

It's important to read titles on graphs. This data is just about women — it doesn't apply to the whole population.

% of female population — Age Groups: 18-24, 25-34, 35-44, 45-54, 55-59, 60-64, 65 and over

1970 / 2001

The data will be about a Citizenship topic you've studied — but you don't have to know anything about Citizenship to answer the question. You need to <u>just</u> use evidence from the graph.

Put a (ring) around the true statement below. **[1]**

(i) Women aged 65 and older were most likely to vote in 2001. This was also the peak for 1970.
This is true for 2001, but 55-59 was the peak for voting in 1970.

(ii) The youngest groups of women have seen the biggest fall in percentage voting turnout between 1970 and 2001.
The graph agrees — women aged 18-34 were much less likely to vote in 2001 than in 1970. The change was far less dramatic in the older age groups.

(iii) The percentage voting turnout has fallen in all age groups of women between 1970 and 2001.
This isn't true for the 65 and over age group. The percentage voter turnout has risen in that age group.

(iv) Women were more likely to vote in the 20th century than they are in the 21st century.
The graph only tells you about 1970 and 2001 — not about women throughout the centuries. You can't draw this conclusion from the graph.

Do Well in Your Exam

Do Well in Your Exam

The grand finale of the exam will be some sort of <u>essay question</u> worth a fair few marks. So don't launch straight into it — have a quick poke around the old memory box first and round up the points you'll use. Scribble down the <u>key words</u>, decide on the best <u>order</u> to put them in, then you can get on with your <u>answer</u>.

You'll Need to *Weigh Up* the *Pros and Cons* of a *Point of View*

You might be asked to discuss how much you <u>agree</u> or <u>disagree</u> with a statement. For example:

> *** The global community**
>
> "Giving short-term humanitarian aid is a waste of the government's money."
>
> Do you agree? Give reasons for your opinion, showing that you have considered **another point of view**.
>
> [12]
>
> Consider the following points as well as **other** information of your own:
> • What responsibilities does the UK government have towards other countries?
> • How effective is humanitarian aid compared to other types of aid?
> • Which global organisations does the UK belong to that deal with humanitarian issues?

Make sure you include everything you're meant to in your answer — ticking the points off as you go is a good idea.

Giving short-term humanitarian aid means providing money or resources to help countries cope with emergencies such as earthquakes or wars.

One way to start off is to define the thing you are talking about.

I disagree that giving short-term humanitarian aid is a waste of money. The government has a moral responsibility to uphold the human rights of people across the world, e.g. their basic right to life, food and shelter. So it has a duty to provide humanitarian aid in response to an emergency. This type of aid has an immediate impact, helping more people to survive the crisis.

Say clearly whether you agree or disagree with the statement. It doesn't matter which point of view you take, as long as you explain it well.

Refer to Citizenship ideas where possible — e.g. 'moral responsibilities' and 'human rights'.

However, some people might argue that giving humanitarian aid does not help the country to develop and become able to cope with future problems. It might also make it reliant on aid. This is why the Department for International Development spends most of its money on long-term <u>divelopment</u> development projects.

Don't forget to give another point of view.

The * next to the question means that you're getting marked on your written communication — so make sure your spelling, punctuation and grammar are accurate.

Long-term development projects include things like building wells, schools and hospitals, or teaching people improved farming methods. These things take a while before people start to see the benefits of them. However, they often permanently improve people's living standards and improve the ability of a country to cope with future problems.

You could also have discussed the advantages of debt relief — see page 36.

Stating the facts shows the examiner that you know what you're talking about.

The UK is a member of the UN, so it agreed to the Millennium Goals set in 2000. These aim to improve living standards in poorer countries by 2015. As a wealthy country, the UK is committed to contributing resources to help reach these goals. While development aid is vital for this, humanitarian aid is also important to help countries recover from emergencies.

Sum up your answer with a concluding statement.

Therefore, while short-term aid is often necessary, it should be given alongside long-term development aid.

Jock finished off his breakfast with the conclusion that it was delicious.

And Finally...

If you've got a bit of time left at the end, <u>read through</u> your answers to double-check them.
You might even come up with a <u>cracker</u> of a point to add to an answer.

Thou shalt write clearly...

A large chunk of how well you do in the exam will come down to, well... how good you are at exams. But if exam skills are the mortar, then facts are the bricks. Learning them well and practising questions will pay off in the end.

Glossary & Index

What, a glossary AND an index — yep, two for the price of one... As usual there's the index to find bits in the book, but then we've gone through, picked out the key organisations and terms you need and given you a simple definition — ideal for quickly clearing up a confusion in your mind, or for last-minute revision. We just think of everything.

Glossary & Index

Glossary & Index